A THEOLOGY OF PROCLAMATION

A THEOLOGY OF PROCLAMATION

HUGO RAHNER, S.J.

TRANSLATED BY RICHARD DIMMLER, S.J.,
WILLIAM DYCH, S.J., JOSEPH HALPIN, S.J.,
AND CLEMENT PETRICK, S.J.,
ADAPTED BY JOSEPH HALPIN, S.J.

HERDER AND HERDER

1968
HERDER AND HERDER NEW YORK
232 Madison Avenue, New York 10016

Original edition: *Eine Theologie der Verkündigung,*
Verlag Herder KG, Freiburg im Breisgau.

Library of Congress Catalog Card Number: 67-29677
© 1968 by Herder and Herder, Inc.
Manufactured in the United States

CONTENTS

A THEOLOGY OF PROCLAMATION

CHAPTER ONE

THEOLOGY AND KERYGMA

Our purpose here will be to reflect upon the dogmatic foundations of our priestly mission. The distinguishing mark of pastoral work during the past decades has been the presence of a wide gap between the concepts and theses brought from theology and the immediate work of the pastor. The "school theology" seemed to be a purely scientific study that to a large extent had little practical value. Exegesis seemed to be absorbed in introductory questions, philological discussions, and disputes with the liberal school. Scholastic dogma as presented to us in Latin might well seem to be but subtle philosophizing on the truths of revelation. The individual disciplines themselves were not integrated with one another, with the result that one often left theology with the feeling that it was a large and unavoidable obstacle on the way to ordination and pastoral work that had no organic connection with the latter.

In reaction to this state of affairs there has arisen in our time an ever growing desire to let the objective order which the revealing God placed in the cosmos of his truths become once again a vital element in our thinking and preaching. At the root of all religious movements in our day lies a secret yearning that we could perhaps characterize as a "dogmatic movement."

Therefore, our chief concern in these lectures should be to show how the priest can strive towards the goal of such a dogmatic structure in all his activity by means of the theological knowledge he has acquired.

The ways to this goal are in themselves numerous. We could

9

review here once again our dogmatic concepts and theses with the emphasis on Scholastic clarity. Certainly there are many deficiencies in this regard. The priest should have certain fundamental questions clarified in his own mind by means of clear Scholastic concepts that, however dry, are certainly necessary —for example, the relation of person and nature in the Trinity and in Christ, the relation of substance and accident in the Eucharist, or the definition of attrition. We could make a systematic review of the whole of dogma in one of its classical formulations, such as that of Thomism. In doing this we would be following the order of the historical development of dogma, and we would have the great advantage of giving to our general theological understanding a certain character. In this way we would acquire "that part of mystery which man can understand" which the First Vatican Council spoke of. It would also have the advantage of giving us this general view of theology according to the order of its actual historical (and so to some extent accidental) development. For the historical development is never oriented by the intrinsic, organic finality of the dogmas themselves, but is dependent upon accidental disputes extrinsic to the dogmas, and dependent also on the historically unique and temporally conditioned genius of the great theologians.

For the starting point of our general survey we look to a word coined by the Greek Fathers, *"kerygma,"* which means a preaching of the message. Our aim is to show how this new aspect is related to the familiar way of looking at the whole of theology that is fundamental in our dogmatic textbooks.

Dogmatic theology is "the scientific exposition of the supernatural truths and the events of salvation that are contained in divine revelation in their organic connections and in a systematic unity."[1] Dogma, therefore, is a "science," the reflection of the human mind on the data of revelation. Hence it is dependent on the principles of selection and structure intrinsic to this reflection. God did not give us his revelation in a

---

[1] B. Bartmann, *Lehrbuch der Dogmatik,* I, 7th edition, p. 2.

"system." The system is constructed by reason enlightened by faith. At the beginning (and at no point in the world of pure revelation) there was no system, but only the simple, pre-scientific preaching of the truths of revelation themselves. Therefore, the human mind does not reduce these facts to a system before there has been a rich development of our knowledge of the facts themselves, nor before this reflective development becomes necessary because of denials that arise or attacks that are made against them.

This gives us some idea of the way that dogma developed historically. It did not begin in force until the second half of the second century. Reflection is therefore always subsequent to preaching. It does not begin until reflection upon the unreflective consciousness of the Church in her faith is forced upon her by contrary opinions. Irenaeus fought against the Gnostics, and out of this dispute arose the early Church's teaching on grace. Origen opposed Celsus, and from this dispute arose the first attempt to construct a whole dogmatic theology. Tertullian wrote against Praxeas, Hippolytus against the Monarchianists, and from these writings developed the dogma of the Trinity in its earliest form. Athanasius opposed Arius, the Cappadocians disputed with the Macedonians, and there was developed the classical doctrine of the Trinity, and finally a complete Christology. Augustine opposed Pelagius, and thereby the urgency of the doctrine of auxiliary grace and that of divine election became evident. Scholasticism is an ingenious defense against the dialectics of the eleventh and twelfth centuries, and from it flows the characteristic forms of medieval dogma. The time from Trent until Vatican I, and even until today, is an age of strong anti-Christian tendencies, and this explains the concentration of recent dogma on questions of fundamental theology.

The principles of structure and selection in this kind of dogmatic theology are therefore essentially two: the questions which the scientific and reflective intellect itself brings to the data of revelation; and the questions which are posed by the historical development of heresies.

11

Therefore, dogmatic theology is constructed mainly upon those solemn declarations of the teaching Church which are promulgated in defense against historically occasioned heresies, and as a result the intellectual reconstruction of revelation proceeds unevenly. Many ideas are developed with extraordinary clarity and comprehension as a necessary sequel to the historical course of heresy (for example, the doctrines of actual grace, the hypostatic union, and the eucharistic presence), while others still rest in the deposit of faith, or are just today giving indication of further development. But seen from the organic structure of revelation, some of these latter are more central than the doctrine of actual grace or of the juridical organization of the Church.

Without a doubt these intellectual reconstructions of the faith and its Scholastic exposition were and are absolutely necessary. For the revelation of the Logos presses on primarily and by its very essence towards logical clarity, and the work of the schools guards against the danger of dissolution. The Scholastic theology of the schools is by no means to be equated with aridity and uselessness, but it is rather and much more, in its classical form, sober headiness," that clear sobriety which builds the banks between which the stream of inspiration can flow securely. Today's antipathy towards Scholastic theology stems mostly from a very insufficient knowledge of it and from misguided enthusiasm.

But dogmatic theology in the form in which it has developed historically does not intend to give us the truths of revelation in the form in which they must be preached. Just as we do not use "chemists as cooks" (Newman), so we do not use the theology of the schools in a diluted and watered-down version as preaching. Just as I do not say that the delightful morning dew that appears on the flower after a summer night is H_2O (although that would be perfectly correct), so I cannot win the hearts of men with that fact that sanctifying grace is a physical accident.

Our most important task, therefore, is the reconstruction of our traditional knowledge, the fashioning out of our dog-

12

matic theology what can be of immediate use in performing the great work to which we are called—preaching.

As we indicated above, we will take as the principle of selection for the reconstruction of our theology the concept "kerygma, preaching the message." This concept has two facets. Kerygma is first the simple preaching of the good news. It comes before any system, and it is essentially given in the essence of revelation itself. Kerygma, therefore, is the preaching of revelation as it went forth from the beginning from the mouth of the preacher sent by God, immediately from preacher to men. For since the Word became flesh, salvation is communicated to all ages only in the indissoluble union of preaching and hearing (Rom. 10, 14). The second facet is very closely joined to the first. Kerygma is the good news as it came forth from God's mouth, with the inner structure and in the arrangement in which the Logos himself conceived it in his wisdom.

Kerygma means, therefore: preaching the revealed divine truths according to the structure in which the divine Wisdom conceived and preached them, the very same structure in which the Church from the very beginning preached the divine revelation in her ordinary teaching (as opposed to her extraordinary teaching in dogmatic definitions).

From the historical point of view, then, kerygma considered in its content must preach urgently those truths which God placed in the foreground in the historical economy of his salvation. Hence we must preach first the enormous fact of revelation itself, something forever inconceivable. This means preaching the divine-human economy of salvation in the full meaning of the word "economy"—that is, the function of all events in the world as a "pedagogy towards Christ," the God-man; his incarnation and the death which it entailed; the recapitulation of the world in Christ and the Church, with her inner finality towards the "coming day" when all in all will again be in the presence of the Father. Hence what we are really preaching is the Trinitarian structure of every salvation event. From the Father comes the Logos who, in the Spirit, brings the Church back to the Father.

13

Formally, this means that we must preach in the manner and with the words which God has deigned to preach these things to us. It means to preach with the words and the simplicity of holy Scripture, with the childlike depth of the teaching Church, with the most valued possessions of theology just as they were received into preaching from the very beginning. This preaching is found in the grateful simplicity of patristic theology as it appears in the kerygmatic writings of the Fathers, in Ignatius, Polycarp, Irenaeus, and the other great men of the early Church. It is likewise found in the baptismal instructions and homilies of Cyril of Jerusalem, and in the *Enchiridion* of Augustine, and in the preaching of the early Middle Ages, in Scarapsus of Pirmion and in the sermons of the Pseudo-Boniface. Kerygma means a preaching in the clarity and power of the great Scholastics, and finally, a preaching which fashions itself upon the liturgy and its forms, which were constructed in the classical ages of kerygmatic theology.

How then must this reconstruction take place? Our fundamental law must be that theology is not only a science for us, but also and essentially the message of salvation. This reconstruction presumes as its vital principle of selection the deep realization and consciousness that we are sent as priests to preach this message. This alone would really be enough to enable us to construct with a sure hand a whole from our somewhat disorganized and scattered pieces of dogmatic knowledge (from our notebooks and theses), to acquire for ourselves an over-all view of the entire revelation. This view would certainly turn out to be something with human limitations, but nevertheless it would be the fulfillment in our own spirit of what the divine preacher, the Logos himself, has preached.

Further, this reconstruction is never an affair of the intellect alone, as though there were question here of a new speculative synthesis. It is much more a "theology of the heart," the genuine result of what Thomas called "divine connaturality,"[2] the "gift of wisdom" that is acquired only by praying and living.

[2] *Summa Theologica*, II, 2, q. 45, a. 2, ad 2c.

14

The task of this reconstruction is "properly to savor," not only to know the truth, but to experience it. For that reason the holy priest is surer of success than the merely learned one.

This reconstruction will succeed only if the priest makes a life-long study of the sources of all kerygmatic theology, if he models himself upon the speaking God, if he speaks as his master speaks, hence if his preaching today is revitalized by an ever renewed contact with the tradition in Scripture, the Fathers, the liturgy, and in the writings of the saints of every century. Knowledge of the Scriptures and of patristic theology are the indispensable conditions for a kerygmatic revival.

One final thought might be added to these introductory remarks. Our concern will not be to bring to completion the reconstruction of our theological knowledge that we have been talking about, as though we could as a result take home with us a dogmatic or catechetical cycle of sermons that would be satisfactory. Our concern is at a deeper level than that of practical necessity. We must ourselves be fulfilled, be reconstructed before we approach directly the reconstruction of our preaching, a reconstruction according to circumstances, according to the condition of our hearers, and according to our own capacities—things which are always different and necessarily variable. Therefore, the chief goal of our work is that dogmatic theology regain its fullness and its splendor for ourselves, for our interior life, and for our priestly contemplation. Without it we cannot preach to the "Greeks and Gentiles" as we should. If, therefore, what we say here seems quite theoretical, quite removed from practical application, this is by no means a slipping back again into the theory of the schools, by no means at variance with the distinction we presented between theology and kerygma, by no means a new opinion of the schools which is supposed to be added to the old with confusing novelty. It is rather that "theory" which, as understood by the Fathers and early Church piety, is the foundation for a true preaching of the message. It is the view, the "being known by being seen," the being-filled-with the value and the beauty of dogmatic truths in their mutual connections, from which alone flows the ability to speak

15

of them in such a way that to the faithful who listen to our words and encounter our priestly personality there comes a happy presentiment of the magnificence of divine grace.

Humbly, we preface to this attempt to outline a theology of kerygma the dedication with which the great Athanasius once concluded his wonderful book on the incarnation of the Word.

"This short treatise is dedicated to you, friend of Christ, as a first sketch and draft of a dogmatic teaching about Christ and his divine coming among us. You should use this as an occasion to occupy yourself with the biblical writings. In a real sense bury yourself in them. For in these Scriptures God has spoken and written through men inspired by God. But we too hand on to you for your study what we have learned from these God-inspired teachers who devoted themselves to the study of the Scriptures and have even become martyrs for the divinity of Christ. . . . But the study of Scripture and its true understanding require also a holy way of life, a pure heart, and the Christian virtues, so that in this way the spirit can reach and grasp what it yearns for, insofar as a knowledge about God, the Logos, is attainable by human nature at all. For without a pure mind and the imitation of the lives of the saints no one can understand the language of the saints."[3]

[3] *De Incarnatione,* 56, 57 (*PG* 25, 193; D. 196d).

16

CHAPTER TWO

THE CONCEPT OF REVELATION AS THE ROOT OF KERYGMA

The classical formula of the Church's kerygma begins with the word "credo." For this reason we shall begin our reconstruction with the same word, so that we might search after the vital center from which the truths of revelation can be constructed organically and vitally. Fundamental theology must also begin with the doctrine of revelation, but from another point of view, one that is more concerned with the defense of revelation and with its logical structure, hence more from the viewpoint of dogma. How can we discover the starting point of our reconstruction in the concept of revelation? We find it in the meaning of the first, powerful word, "credo," and in the meaning of the awe-inspiring dialogue in baptism: "What do you seek from the Church? Faith. And what does faith offer you? Eternal life." Belief in the fact of revelation itself, being filled with awe and true fear over this incredible fact, that God has spoken to me, there lies the starting point and the all-penetrating form of our kerygmatic theology. We shall work this out in two steps.

I. THE FACT AND THE CONCEPT OF REVELATION

Natural theology or theodicy knows God's existence and essence from created things, according to the definition of Vatican I. Moreover, as St. Thomas taught, it draws further conclusions about God by the ways of causality, negation, and eminence. Therefore, it knows God only (although with certainty and even with facility) as the final cause of created things, as the ultimate meaning of creation, as the one who possesses everything true, good, and beautiful in creatures and has them to an eminent degree and without limitation. God becomes known as the ultimate cause of the world. All of this knowledge from natural theology about God possesses God only as the personal, transcendent cause of the individual object of human knowing, as cause of the world. It never possesses himself as object, as one who could be approached independently of his relation to the world.

But what, or better, who God is in himself, what he intends in the depths of his uncreated freedom precisely as a free person, as we know him to be by our natural knowledge, what he wishes or desires, none of this can I know from "natural" revelation. I can know this only when this free God speaks to me, when he deigns to break through the silence of his creation with his Word, when he pulls back the veil which necessarily lies over the mystery of his interior personality (as over every person, even the created), when he *re-velat,* when he permits an apocalypse, an absolutely spontaneous handing over of himself to the knowledge of the creature. But when such a divine communication occurs, this Word of God necessarily demands from the creature an absolute consent. Hence revelation is never merely a divine narrative involving no obligation on our part. Rather, this loving spontaneity of the divine self-surrender corresponds necessarily to the inevitable obligation in the creature to hear and to act. Revelation, then, is "the word of God as a witness." God speaks, giving testimony to himself, and therefore he demands consent. We must attend to the fullness of this dry-sounding definition, savor it to the full, fill ourselves with it. This speaking of God is a perfectly free act which proceeds only from love. For love is ever a revelation of the most secret, a surrender of one person to another, a creative giving, that is, one without a reason, due to the initiative of the giver alone. Therefore the Church emphasizes in the First Vatican

Council the powerful word *"placuit"* (D. 1785) with regard to revelation: "to have pleased his wisdom and goodness."

It is therefore of fundamental importance for the priest that he enter ever more deeply into this incredible fact, that God wanted to tell us something about himself, that he be gripped by this fact as by something that at once perplexes and gives joy. It is important that he read in holy Scripture the deepest meaning that his office has. He is called to go and to preach in the world in the name of this speaking God (his experience is that of the prophet), and to learn to hear the speaking of God through intensive study of Scripture so that he can repeat it to others.

A revelation of naturally knowable things was possible and useful, but by no means absolutely necessary (D. 1786); the fact of revelation becomes meaningful only from the viewpoint of mystery. Man becomes a mystic, one initiated into the mysteries of God's person, a sharer in the knowledge of the Holy Spirit (D. 1795). The content of revelation is therefore not just an increase in knowledge guaranteed by divine authority, a knowledge that in itself would be accessible to clever human reasoning also, but it is an essentially different kind of knowledge (Vatican I calls it "distinct in principle and object"). It is knowledge in faith of that truth which is hidden in God, knowledge of the interior personality of God himself which some day we shall see. Revelation is therefore made intelligible from an eschatological viewpoint, from its finality: the vision of the Trinity.

We should speak much more frequently to the faithful about revelation. They must know and become aware of the fact that the priest is concerned with deep mysteries, that he comes from out of the wilderness where he was burdened with the weight of his mission, to speak in God's name, to be a prophet. They must realize that Christianity is not just another religion which serves to help one to carry the miseries of life a little better and which also speaks occasionally of things hereafter. Revelation is the basic reason for our priestly mission and the justification of our claim to be heard. It is the Lord who bids us

19

to speak. This is also the reason why we must labor ardently throughout our lives to acquire an ever deeper knowledge of the truths of revelation. We cannot allow one iota of the kerygma to go unheard, nor can we, on the basis of some psychological ground, make a selection of the truths of revelation that seem to us contemporary. For not a crumb of the divine bread which we must break can be lost.

II. THE CONCEPT OF REVELATION AS THE ROOT OF THE KERYGMATIC RECONSTRUCTION OF OUR PREACHING

Revelation is a speaking by God, but always a speaking to men, whose spirit always reaches the world through the senses. Revelation is always a speaking in a spiritual-sensible form, for the spiritual-material person of man can receive God's word in no other way. Hence revelation is always extended in space and time, it is always historical, and yet it is necessarily in its inner nature (since it is the word of God) invisible, spiritual, eternal. This is seen best in the One who is God's prophet in the fullest sense: the Word become flesh. "It was spoken in the Son," and indeed, "most recently in those days" (Heb. 1, 2). The revelation of God become flesh is an indissoluble unity of the historically visible, the other-wordly, the divine. This mystery of the hypostatic union communicates itself to the whole of God's revelation, extending backward to the first word of Genesis and the whole economy of salvation in the Old Testament, extending forward to the last day in the history of the development of this revelation, in the divine-human structure of the Church, her priesthood, and her history. Revelation is always and necessarily clothed in sensible, perceptible words, though it is in itself a purely spiritual and eternal truth. Every exaggerated emphasis on one or the other of these components would lead to a falsification, to mysticism or rationalism. It would make of God's word either a kind of gnosis or a teaching of the man Jesus that has but human beauty and purity. Only in the

20

Church are spirit and word constantly maintained, and our preaching today must fashion itself on the kerygma of the Church, maintaining the historically sensible and the spiritually eternal of revolution. Two lines thus become clear from this attempt to lay the foundation of the concept of revelation, and these lines will show us the way to a kerygmatic division of the truths of revelation.

We could derive this foundation for kerygmatics from the concept of revelation from still another point of view. Revelation is always a communication of knowledge and being. It is faith and new life. This new life begins with faith as its starting point, and, vice versa, faith is the activity of this new way of life, the activity of supernatural being. But this new life is a participation in the life of the Trinity (and so also participation in the knowledge about this life), hence in the eternal, spiritual life of God. But it is participation in and through Christ, the God-man, in his spatio-temporal being and its development in Church and sacrament. There result from this point of view the two lines of the spiritual and the visible which permit us now to comprehend the structure of kerygma.

The spiritual and invisible line: Trinity, elevation of the creature to union with the Trinity, original sin, hypostatic union, mystical body of the Church, the sanctifying grace of Christ, beatific vision of the Trinity.

The spatio-temporal, historically visible line: life of Christ, visible Church, visible priesthood, sacraments, resurrection of the flesh, the new earth.

These two lines are never separated, nor do they develop side by side with one another, but they interpenetrate, as in the inimitable prototype of the hypostatic union where divine and human nature unite in a single person.

Really they are not lines but circles, which proceed from the Trinitarian God and return to him (as the words of Eccl. 1, 7, so beloved by the mystics, indicate: "the rivers return to that place from which they stemmed"). This is the way the Fathers of the Church constructed their kerygma, as is best and most deeply shown in the *Epideixis* of Irenaeus: the Father as

21

first beginning and happy end, Christ as the great mediator, the Church as his Body, which together with the Head returns to the Father.

In this way revelation will become for the priest as preacher a structure, a powerful drama, with all the individual truths which make up the whole being recapitulated in a single kerygma, the message of the divinization of man through the incarnation of God.

CHAPTER THREE

TRINITY AS BEGINNING AND END OF THE INVISIBLE

We begin in this chapter (and will continue on through the sixth) to treat of the revealed truths which we characterized as the invisible line, those truths which form, as it were, the soul of revelation. We shall follow that order which is perhaps best suited for a kerygmatic and organic construction of the facts of our belief. In doing so we do not deny that another arrangement is possible in a kerygmatic approach to these truths. In the matter of structure there is room for a great deal of freedom. Even great saints have personally preferred other groupings than the one here presented. In their very effective preaching they placed many truths in a psychologically central place which does not belong to them in the objective order. J. A. Jungmann in his book *Die Frohbotschaft und unsere Glaubensverkündigung* arranges the truths from a human and psychological point of view, rather than in that ontological arrangement which is adhered to especially in Scholastic dogmatic theology.

However, we feel that today there is a strong tendency to retain the objective order even for preaching, not only because the "school theology" constructs it in this way, but also because in revelation itself, especially in Paul, this arrangement predominates. In any case, before he begins his preaching, which certainly has to be adapted to needs, the priest must fill himself completely with the beauty, the peace, and the inner power of a total conception of the divine revelation, and this can be acquired only by a prayerful, over-all view and a thinking

23

through of the whole economy, the total order of divine salvation. Only then is he in a position to accomplish the necessary adaptation in any given situation with theological accuracy and pastoral relevance.

The starting point in our arrangement is thus the mystery of the holy Trinity which is the beginning and the happy ending of the invisible line.

There is no doubt that for us today this most Christian of all Christian realities has yielded its central place in our preaching. In the great ages of Christianity this was not the case.

Nevertheless, we must ask ourselves how it was possible in the early ages of Christianity that not only this or that theologian and Father but the consciousness of the Christian community as such was so passionately involved in the Trinitarian dispute. How much kerygmatic instruction of the people is presupposed by the gigantic battle against Arianism, how vital was the feeling that it was the fundamentals of Christianity that were at stake in the case of Arius and that of Macedonius! What a task it would be—it is as yet not done—to show how, in the anti-Arian movement in Spain, in Merovingian Gaul until the time of the early German mission, the preaching of Christianity devoted itself with great urgency to this central mystery. Or to show how our forefathers of the seventeenth century still had a living knowledge of the mystery of the Trinity and gave it expression in baroque art.

In contrast to this fullness stands our own emptiness, which precisely on this point suffers from the hollowness of the age of the Enlightenment. Certainly the Trinity is an article of our faith exactly as it always has been in the Church. But how insipid has the kerygmatic exploitation of this truth become. There still remains the "loving Father in heaven," almost with a deistic undertone, and the heavenly Father in the tabernacle. Regrettably, the word "Father" is in many cases only the expression for a very sentimentally imagined providence. The Holy Spirit is the unknown God, or he is praised as Something new in a strangely unconnected devotion to the Holy Spirit. Usually, then, there remains only the humanity of Christ, and even the

24

deepest mystery of this human heart, his passionate love for the Father, is emasculated, reduced almost to what the liberal Christologies of the Harnack school made out of it.

Nevertheless (this is always a profound good fortune in the living, developing Church), the forms, prayers, and customs of the ages of the great Trinitarian kerygma have been preserved. We still possess them, and have only to fill them with new spirit, a thing which itself is traditional in the Church. We still pray at the beginning of every prayer, "In the name of the Father," and we still say the doxology. We speak of this mystery whenever we bless and preach and console. We know that the words which express this mystery are raised to sacramental power in baptism, in penance, and in confirmation. Our preaching of the mysteries must take as its point of departure this sublime treasure of prayer: "the law of praying, the law of believing." How, then, should this kerygma of the Trinity be formulated?

I. THE MYSTERY IN ITSELF

The preaching of the mysteries must proceed in the way in which God himself has deigned to speak of them. Our kerygma must be an imitation of the divine kerygma precisely in this case where there is question of the interior mystery of God. But this means that we must not begin with the speculation with which (necessarily) theology begins, above all in defense of the early medieval dialectic, and develops the knowledge of this mystery. But we must preach this central mystery with the same urgency and the same divine demand of the *"locutio Dei attestans"* with which the Word become flesh spoke of it, who is in the bosom of the Father and who "alone knows who the Father is."

Therefore, it is the indispensable task of the priest to make himself familiar with the divine kerygma of the Trinity from Scripture and Tradition. He must have a sense for the passion of the triune God, who creates in secret, to speak the secrets

25

of his heart to men. This means he must root his deepest idea of Old Testament theology out of the Old Testament, how God from the beginning, one might almost say hesitatingly and shyly (since one always states the deepest things with reserve), began to speak of these things, namely, the primitive revelation, hypostasis theology, and books of wisdom. This means the priest must fill himself above all with the brilliantly clear way in which Jesus speaks of the Father and the Spirit, holding him, the Father, as the only passion of his heart. At this point there is certainly possible an unspeakably beautiful and just as unspeakably necessary deepening of the theology of the Sacred Heart. The priest must make clear to himself that the passion of this human heart for the Father is nothing but the human echo of the burning love which for all eternity is exchanged in the bosom of the Father through the Holy Spirit. Then all the words of Jesus about the Father receive a very new ring. The priest must place all these words together, must repeat them after Jesus again and again, and he must fashion his own speech after these, must keep wisdom on his lips, must be passionately filled with the thought that he is sent to tell men: "this is eternal life, that they recognize the Father and he whom he sent, Jesus Christ."

This means that he must familiarize himself with the Trinitarian structure of the Pauline theology, that he must trace these truths in St. John, since they are fundamental there too (as in the earliest beginnings of the Christian kerygma). Our theology must once again become more biblical. Then will we be able to speak also of the fundamental mystery of holy Scripture. This means, finally, that the priest must educate himself in Tradition better than he has done in the past, in the patristic way of speaking of the Trinity. Who has formed himself in the sublime theology of Ignatius and Irenaeus? Who has really ever read the forever fresh work of Athanasius on the incarnation of the Logos? We do not realize that they are, so to speak, things of luxury for the spiritual gourmet. The most simple people have a wonderful capacity for this mystery (certainly because the infused gift of faith is given at the moment when the soul is created anew with the words: "I baptize you in the name of the Father"). Relying upon this capacity, we must form ourselves with the kerygmatic literature of the Fathers indicated in our first chapter. We must ask ourselves the question, "How was the Trinity spoken of in past ages in the baptismal instruction?" Today we speak around this mystery almost timidly lest we disturb men's thinking. Classically formed Christianity loved to speak of the Trinity. Even in the great Scholastics, above all in Thomas, there is much more than speculation to be found. There is an affectionate speaking about the deepest things which we have received as the gift from the depths of God. How deeply St. Ignatius of Loyola was penetrated with this mystery! If his Exercises are made correctly, or, what is often the case, given correctly, they are clearly an introduction into Trinitarian theology and mysticism.

Further, the preaching of the mystery of the Trinity must —insofar as it is true that it must make the same claims and demands as revelation itself—go into what theology calls the divine processions. For as much as the mystery of the Trinity is hidden from us in faith, God has nevertheless deigned to give us even in this life a secret and wonderful insight into the deepest essence of the divine persons. It is a great error when one is so rash as to consider anything connected with the Trinity as mere scientific speculation and so exclude it from the kerygma. The fact of the matter is (as will be shown later) that we, too, cannot speak appropriately, and with theological perspective of the mystery of our own divinization, if we do not know how to speak of the divine processions. For how are we going to speak of sonship without speaking of the Father and his only Son? How are we going to speak of the spiritual life without speaking of the Spirit?

Let us begin with the first procession: the Son is generated by the Father.

At this point there arises one of the most difficult kerygmatic problems. If we want to speak of the Trinity with theological accuracy, we must be able to say accurately what the divine

27

persons are. We must formulate accurately (in various ways, according to the degree of education of the men to whom we are preaching the "good news") what we are going to say when someone asks us, "Why and how is God a person? What are the divine persons?" Today, when there is more concern than ever for the correct understanding of the "personal" God, this truth cannot be for us a half-understood acquisition from Greek philosophy, which certainly serves to some extent to distinguish difficulties ("one nature, three persons"); we must take the trouble to acquire from philosophy and from experience, with conceptual clarity and also with the spiritual impetus of love, a full understanding of what person means. This is indeed one of the most difficult pieces of our kerygmatic reconstruction of theology. Joseph Scheeben tried to do it in his *The Mysteries of Christianity*,[1] but he was not completely successful because his language was all too often merely a translation of the Latin of the schools. We must in our preaching about person proceed from the Latin *"subsistentia"* or the Greek *"hypostasis,"* and show how in these words is expressed that which is subsistent in its own being, independent in its origin, with its ultimate foundation in its own essence, which we connect with the word "person." We must try to show how there necessarily corresponds to created spiritual nature a personal existence, how in personality the most precious of all things is expressed, a thing given through the Spirit, the royalty and likewise (as we know from revelation alone) the limitation of the spiritual, created person. We must try to show how this externally peaceful self-possession of the divine nature rests in three persons, but that the created nature necessarily is created in one person. We could still further draw rich suggestions from the way in which the Fathers (above all, after the theology of the Cappadocians and St. Augustine) sought to bring this mystery nearer to understanding from the *vestigia Trinitatis* in the human spirit. Michael Schmaus has shown this in a comprehensive way in his fine work, *Die psychologische Trinitätslehre des hl. Augustinus.*

---

[1] *Mysterien des Christentums*, Mainz, 1931, pp. 62–66 (ET *The Mysteries of Christianity*, St. Louis, 1946).

Now to the procession of the Son himself. Our preaching must be deeply penetrated with the reverence with which the great Fathers ventured to speak of this mystery. Non-Christians must at least suspect that we speak here of the original source of our Christianity, that redemption, Church, state of grace, sonship, resurrection of the flesh, exist and are blessed realities only because the Father eternally generates the Son: "Today I have begotten you." For the sake of the divine depths of our own sonship, it must be shown how creation and generation are different. We must try to exhaust the depths of the definition of generation: "the origin of a living from a living joined in a similitude of nature," hence what truly mystical blessedness lies in the words "from a living joined." The early Fathers drew the same truth from the words of St. John (1, 18): "the Son who is in the bosom of the Father." They have fashioned from these words their striking theology of the Son proceeding from the heart of the Father, this true "theology of the heart" which spoke of the Word which overflowed from the heart of the Father, which sang of this outpouring of love in hymns and antiphons: "the heart born from its parent prior to the beginning of the world." It is here that Augustinian piety has its foundations. This piety continued until the mysticism of the Middle Ages and there released all the riches of Trinitarian mysticism, in the "eternally generated" Son, in the "today" of the psalm: "Today I have begotten you." Here did the theology of Clement of Alexandria (*Ped. I,* 5–6) receive its stimulus to speak of the "Child of the Father." It is preserved until the time of the art of the Russian icons, where the Logos-Child appears, and where in the accompanying theology the mystery of our sonship is joined with the mystery of the sonship of God in quite another way than by us. Or we keep simply to the word of the Church as it is expressed with unsurpassable clarity by the Fourth Lateran Council: "The Son from the Father alone, and the Holy Spirit equally from both: without a beginning, eternal and without end." In the Fourth Lateran Council we have an example of how the kerygma of the Church itself can teach in words which we too must preach. Against

29

the errors of the Abbot Joachim the dogma of the Trinity is expounded with striking clarity. When well translated these sentences are a sermon on the Trinity since they have that power and clarity which penetrated every age of the Church which defended this basic mystery. Should this be so forgotten in our time—not forgotten, of course, in the convictions of our faith, but all too often in the vitality of our preaching?

We come now to the procession of the Holy Spirit, and we must strive for a more exact penetration into the meaning of the *filioque*. This doctrine is not only the result of dogmatic speculation and the long and rather subtle disputes of Greek minds. For as soon as a truth becomes a clearly defined dogma, part of the faith, it is no longer speculation or irrelevant theologoumenon; by the fact of definition we have a guarantee that the truth is revealed, that it stands in living and vitalizing relation to our lives and so deserves that we meditate upon it with reverence and faith, since it is now seen to be a part of the totality of the divine drama of revelation. Such is the case with the *filioque*. In this dogma lie the basic reasons why the grace of sonship is a "spiritual" life, why our bodies will rise in the spiritualizing power of this life, since this body is the body of the Son of God, or better—since it is the body of the brother of Christ—the brother of him who rose in the power of the paternal Spirit. The Spirit is the Spirit of Christ, and therefore everything which we subsequently conclude from this dogma is given fundamentally in this powerful truth, that the Spirit proceeds from the Father and the Son. The kerygmatic emphasis on this fact is also of great importance because only in this way can a special devotion to the Holy Spirit be based upon theological and especially kerygmatic correctness (which two are not always the same). This truth, at once clear and mysterious, of the one procession of the Spirit from both Father and Son gives us some idea how the Holy Spirit is the common and unifying element in the interior life of God, the fragrance and the force of the relation of Father to Son —the homeland, so to speak, in whose haven and embrace the divine love flourishes. From this point of view we can see how in the divine work of salvation *ad extra,* which is certainly common to the three Persons insofar as the one divine nature is the efficient cause of the creation of grace, the interior divine relations are mirrored and mysteriously imitated. Consequently, in our kerygmatic theology there should be not so much a devotion to the Holy Spirit as a new devotion of the interior life—but much more, and more urgently than before, a spiritualization of the work of Christ. This means, in the sense of the theology of Paul, a deepened appreciation of how the Spirit descended upon men from the Father through Christ as a formative principle and as the foundation of the Church, of sanctifying grace, and of final glorification. We must give much more emphasis to the Trinitarian structure of the whole work of the economy. We must, to express it paradoxically, give honor to the Holy Spirit precisely by looking to the Father through the Son. For the Holy Spirit is not just another divine person (so that we simply take the number three as something given, almost with the half-conceived notion that there could just as well be two or four persons), but the person who is love, in whom the Father embraces his essence uttered in the Logos in and through this image of himself. Thus the imitation through grace of this inner, divine, metaphysical necessity of the relationship of the Spirit to the Son-Father must in like manner be directed to the divine rhythm of the *filioque.*

In our kerygmatic language we must become more familiar than before with the precious depths of the language about the Holy Spirit which has been sanctified and consecrated by tradition (and on this point Scheeben in his *The Mysteries of Christianity* is an excellent example, as in general are all those theologians whose thought has been enriched by Greek patristic theology). The dogma of the Holy Spirit (and we say this with all reverence) is really the poetry, the lyric of revelation, and therefore in every age the majesty of the *Veni Creator Spiritus* or the intimacy of the *Veni Sancte Spiritus* has gripped hearts with great force, precisely as did the majestic Spirit-psalm 103 in the original revelation. The entire office of the feast of Pentecost is a poem of mystic depths. Since the third

31

person in God is Spirit, hence impetus, inspiration, fire, ecstatic jubilation, hence also, though hidden under the veil of the temporal, the penetration into the deepest part of us by "poetry and prayer," as Bremond calls it, therefore we shall all some-day, when death has penetrated into life, be mystics, ecstatic and joyful poets (if we can speak in this way), full of the Spirit, filled with the "sober headiness" of him who in God has per-sonal jubilation. Should nothing of all this be experienced in our preaching on this earth? Does it not at this point become clear that this kerygmatic jubilation must constantly be based upon and formed by the sobriety of true theology, by the severe sobriety of believing wisdom (for the Holy Spirit is ever the Spirit of the Logos), but also that it is more urgent that our kerygma be again filled with the inspiration of the Holy Spirit, so that today as in the past the world thinks that "they are drunk"?

II. THE MYSTERY OF THE DIVINE PROCESSIONS IN ITS RELATION TO US

We have treated sketchily of our relationship to the Trinity, but it is now time to treat it systematically. We must begin our preaching of the Trinity with a feeling of astonishment that the Trinity has ventured to hand itself over so completely to creatures, to surrender the innermost mystery of its heart, and this because of a love which the incarnate Word calls friend-ship and theology calls the love of benevolence ("To you I have said that I heard from the Father"). St. Thomas Aquinas commented in the *Summa Contra Gentiles:* "It is proper to friendship that the friend reveal his secrets to some-one: for friendship joins the affections of two people making them as one. It does not seem a betrayal to have mentioned something revealed by a friend, as when the Lord told his disciples: I shall not call you servants..."[2]

[2] IV, 21

32

We are, therefore, brought into the very core of the Trinitarian life by the communication of this mystery to creatures. God communicated this mystery to us because he wanted to draw us close to his innermost heart (St. Ignatius of Loyola), and likewise he drew us into this participation in the divine life since otherwise we would not be able to grasp and bear the mystery of this divine heart. So the mystery of the Trinity becomes the prototype and the essential structure of our own divinization. We cannot understand the meaning of our own state of grace and of the whole economy of divine salvation without seeing this Trinitarian structure as its foundation. The Church has made this structure the basis of her divinization in a classic way in her own kerygma, in the Apostles' Creed.

This creed is structured according to the Trinitarian creedal formula. Its structure is preserved for us most clearly (still without the kerygma of the incarnate Word added somewhat later) in the baptismal formula of the papyrus from Dei-Balizek:

> *I believe in God, the Father, the Almighty,*
> *And in his only-begotten Son*
> *Our Lord Jesus Christ,*
> *And in the Holy Spirit,*
> *And in the resurrection of the flesh,*
> *And in the holy Catholic Church.*[3]

The structure of the whole economy is here articulated with striking clarity. Our belief proceeds from that which in God is origin and blessed end, the Father. The Creed begins not with a confession of one God (belief in one God was taken for granted), but with the confession of this one God as he who is the Father of an only Son. And the Son is our Lord, who bore the singly earthly name Jesus and is the Christ who is anointed by the Spirit, anointed by the Spirit who likewise is the God of my faith. In Christ, the Father and the Spirit have come to us. This will finally be apparent in the resurrection of the flesh. And there will be a resurrection because the Holy

---

[3] *Texte und Untersuchungen,* 36, 1b (1910), pp. 30 ff.; see *Zeitschrift für katholische Theologie,* 48 (1924), p. 465.

33

Spirit brought the divine life of the Spirit, the "spiritual" life, down upon earth through Christ, in that community which is for this reason called the "holy" Church. The Church, therefore, is the fulfillment on earth of that which the Spirit is in God. It is the saving homeland in which the sanctification of men is fulfilled through Christ until the spiritualized, glorious resurrection "in the holy Church." Therefore, "Church" is the mystical circle which connects the end with the beginning, the return home with the original source, with the Father from whose bosom the Son proceeded, in order to bring sons home, which is what the "being called together" of the Church means. The Church is an imitation of the Spirit, who unites the Father and Son in love. Church and Spirit: they belong together since Pentecost, the significance of which for the economy of salvation becomes clear only against the background of the Trinity. "We believe in eternal life through the holy Church," says an African creed. And in the Syrian consecration of a bishop (still used today in the West Syrian rite) the "faithful dogma of the Trinity through the cross, through the resurrection, and through the incorruptibility in the holy Church of God," is laid on the head of the bishop-elect. Is this not the deepest formulation of everything that we want to bring home to our own hearts in priestly kerygma?

There are two dogmatic truths of our faith which in a special way cannot be preached correctly except upon the foundation of the Trinitarian kerygma. They are the truth of the hypostatic union and the truth of the grace of sonship. We shall speak of these two truths separately in the coming chapters, which from now on will simply be developments of what has been here touched upon briefly.

CHAPTER FOUR

THE MYSTERY OF ORIGINAL JUSTICE AND ORIGINAL SIN

We pursue now the history of the overflowing of divine Trinitarian life into the realm of creatures, according to the structure which results from our concept of revelation. We will meditate on the extension of the interior divine processions into the creature, in whom the same God imprints the image of his Son so that he partakes in his own divine nature, and by so doing gives birth again to his own Son in the creature. He breathes his own Spirit into the creature and draws it into his inner, supernatural community of love.

Our first question, therefore, in this construction of our kerygmatic organism concerns the great mystery of the supernatural elevation of man, and likewise the equally profound mystery of his original fall. This matter includes original justice and original sin. Only from this point of view do we get any insight into this deepest mystery, at least in the actual plan of the divine message of salvation. This plan involves the extension of the interior divine life into a completely determinate individual creature, into the human nature of the God-man in the hypostatic union, and into the restoration, following upon this union, of the whole race in the bringing home to the heart of the Father. This new unity is recreated in the people of God—that is, Church, those who are called together.

The dogmas of the supernatural and of original sin must be incorporated fully and forcefully into our consciousness in faith, and hence into our preaching. Otherwise everything that we preach remains to a certain extent in an area that is morally consoling and edifying, but dealing merely with this world. Our preaching would then necessarily be lacking its very heart, the source of all its force and all its inspiration that transcends the world. The low level of the Church's kerygma in the age of the Enlightenment, when the supernatural and original justice and original sin were evaporated (or appeared relegated far into the background), is frightening evidence of the truth of our remarks.

Kleutgen and Scheeben saw this possibility with ingenious insight when they established relations again with such great theological forefathers as Patavius, Ripalda, Suarez, and Thomas. Augustine fought against Pelagianism with passionate clarity. Still earlier the great forerunners of the Catholic doctrine on the supernatural—Irenaeus, Clement of Alexandria, and even Ignatius the martyr—consciously developed the dogma of the supernatural and demonstrated it from the sources of our faith against the mystical naturalism of the Gnostics. The Gnostics destroyed the foundations of the Christian revelation about the elevation of man by grace to participation in the divine nature by their lofty yet superficial progress of the soul to the heights of gnosis.

This magnificent battle of the spirit, which was waged from the days of Gnosticism through Palagius and down to the rational dialecticians of the early Middle Ages, and from then down to Baius and the superficiality of the Enlightenment which was the final result of Baius, is still being waged in our time, when there is an inclination to level, to a certain extent, the supernatural down to a new happiness of human culture. Hence we must continue the fight, and we must fight with a clarity about this true article of divine revelation that glows with love, in a tireless preaching of the dogma of the supernatural, and of all that is inseparable from it, original sin and redemption given again in Christ. For we can never say: "I believe in eternal life" if we have not understood at the beginning of our creed the divine origin of this eternal life.

Hence we must speak here about the manner of our preaching the doctrine of the supernatural in general, and of the doctrine of the original justice of the human race and original sin.

I. THE DOCTRINE OF THE SUPERNATURAL

There is more lively discussion about this question today than there ever was, for the ideas of enlightened rationalism are still having their aftereffects everywhere, only now in modern dress. We find it, for example, in the doctrine of the fundamental and final values of humanity, which recognizes no others beyond those of the individual or the collectivity. Opposed to these values are the excessive subtleties of dialectical theology, which stem from the "mere" and naked supernaturalism of Calvin. These preach an other-worldly Christianity that is suspended, as it were, without roots, and in which the human signifies only a contradiction to everything divine. They deny everything that we shall treat as the visible line of the whole revelation in the coming chapters. Here our preaching must preserve from the outset the human-divine center of Catholic revelation.

We will begin with a few false and too limited notions of the supernatural. The supernatural is in the final analysis nothing but the great mystery of man, which is more clearly shown to us through divine revelation. It is one's essence as creature in the relation to God rooted in his very depths. Hence in itself it is nothing more than a relation to God in the creature, more easily and surely known through revelation. Or the supernatural is the totality of the effects of divine help, which are necessary to lead a morally good life. This was a very popular way of speaking in the catechisms of the eighteenth century, when there was so much joy in the peaceful and beautiful idyll of man's innocent nature. Grace is considered as a healing of the moral defects of man (proceeding from the opposite pole, the assumption of the absolute corruption of human nature through original sin). The supernatural is equated with useful

37

benefits and is considered to be owed to man. "Good" is nothing but the supernatural—wherefore the supernatural is owed to the human creature that originally came from God's hand; it belongs to his human endowment. Finally, there results from this view, contrary to its known intention, a naturalism of the grossest kind: "it is absurd to consider that man was, from the outset, raised beyond the state of his nature to the supernatural by a certain gratuitous gift" (Baius, Prop. 23; D. 1023). It would not be very difficult to show that many of the opinions still current today curiously unite in themselves the naturalism based on "the pure and beautiful nature of man" and the naturalism corresponding to the subtle supernaturalism of Baius. Even today Baius is still strikingly alive.

Between these extremes, which are found over and over again in unexpected surroundings, is the genuine Catholic preaching of the supernatural. There are few points in our kerygmatic where it is shown more clearly that only the clarity of the scientific Scholastic concepts can give to our enthusiasm the "savoring of sobriety."

We must now introduce, for the sake of clarity in our preaching on the supernatural (and this is not in educated circles, but also in simple sermons), the so-called doctrine of the "state of human nature." In order to explain the perfect supernaturality of the end to which God's love has called us and the whole human race, it must be shown that God could also have created man in a state of pure nature (D. 1055). This is to counteract a leveling of the supernatural which has ever been current since Baius, Hermes, and Günther. However, our preaching must also make it clear that God never effectively willed this "pure nature"; that, seen historically, there is only one state of human nature, the state of man supernaturally elevated, in which all are called to one life which essentially transcends nature.

This must become so clear that a merely natural fulfillment of man "no longer has at all the character of a desirable and realizable goal," as Scheeben says. Catholic doctrine teaches that nature is created and bestowed by God only so that it might serve as substratum and as an organ of supernatural life.[1] It is precisely this fact that is of such fundamental importance in our preaching today. From this fact it must be shown that there are not two spheres, no double destiny, as it were, for men, no merely secular sphere and then besides a sacral, ecclesiastical, supernatural sphere. There is no "pure human nature" in the whole enormously long history of human millenniums. For this reason, human nature, without the supernatural, cannot even achieve the purely human, this-worldly perfection that would otherwise belong to it. All culture without grace is, according to Augustine, only another form that the *"splendida peccata"* of worldliness takes. All of this must be preached certainly with the theological and pastoral prudence which remains conscious of the extraordinary ways of divine salvation and does not become blind to the noble and lofty values of humanity, even of pagans. But all this must not degenerate into an attempt to compromise the heroic uniqueness of the divine will for salvation. It must not make a Catholic ghetto out of God's economy of grace, where man can "also" be happy, exactly in the same way, or at the most a little more easily as in many other ways, and each according to his own way. With respect to this absolute character of grace, based on the theology of the Fathers and without which we do not have a true understanding of the Church, mission, or the obligation to preach the word which weighs upon us (1 Cor. 9,16), there remains, even for all truly good things which happen "outside" the Church, the word of the Council of Orange (D. 195): "If man possesses truth and justice, he takes it from that fountain which we ought to thirst for in this life." Both the humility and the pride of the Catholic consciousness could be founded in this statement.

Beginning with this doctrine on the state of human nature the theological center of our preaching on the supernatural can now be correctly presented. We proceed in this instance also from the point of view worded out in the dogmatic tradi-

[1] Matthias J. Scheeben, *Handbuch der katholischen Dogmatik,* II, Freiburg, 1933, pp. 428, 432.

39

tion. The supernatural must first be conceived (to use the language of the schools) from the viewpoint of its *terminus a quo,* the nature of man. We all know the definition. The supernatural is that gift of God to the nature of the human creature "which neither constitutively, nor consecutively, nor exigently pertains to any created nature." Theology thus conceives the essence of what it calls supernatural *simpliciter.* We must now reconstruct this essence kerygmatically and try to express it in a form that can be preached. This definition contains striking praise of human nature, a recognition of all that the Creator has bestowed upon the nature of man (and of every other spiritual creature, hence the angels), a nature which itself is an image of God. It is, therefore, by no means the case that the splendor of our knowledge of the supernatural entails a diminution or belittling of nature in order that the former be understood in its beauty. To bring out the essence of the supernatural, we must first sing the praises of nature, we must show how everything natural, up to the striking heights of genius and the artistic, of personal and historical values and conquests, really belongs to nature, to that which belongs to a spiritual creature as sequel or enriching addition. Only from this point of view can we rightfully allude to the sublime mystery that God has bestowed upon this humanity, so rich and so capable of development, gifts which exceed its nature or what is due to it. Now the stream of our kerygmatic inspiration, drawn only from divine revelation, must break forth. The Trinitarian God, at the beginning of creation, in truth even before the conception of a creation, deigned to raise this future creation (whose nature therefore was destined precisely for this) into the sphere of his own nature, to draw it to his heart, into the inner, personal realm of his own Trinitarian life, to make men "sharers of divine nature." And this no longer through a mere creation, but through a real generation. Here what we saw in the chapter about the Trinity shines forth, how the words "the origin of a living being from a living being of like nature" conceal in their sober expression the whole fire of enrapturing, heart-warming proximity to God exceeding all nature. It is

40

of such a kind that the same proximity to the Father before the morning star now is given to created nature by grace in a mystery understandable only in terms of the Trinity, so that we can grasp this proximity to the Father in the single expression, "sonship in God."

We have now come to the second aspect of the concept of the supernatural, which the theology of the school has developed so masterfully, seeing it from the *"terminus ad quem."* The supernatural means essentially participation in a nature which is higher than the nature of which the supernatural is predicated. Thus the way of knowing which is natural to angels (without a sensible phantasm) would be for men somehow supernatural. In its fullest sense, however, the supernatural is for every creature the participation in the Trinitarian nature of God, since this participation never means mere creation, but a certain extension of the divine processions into the realm of the creature, in which the creature is imprinted with the image of the divine Son—participation after the manner in which the divine persons possess this nature. Hence this human participation is a mysterious fulfillment of the birth and breath of the inner life of God. The great and inexhaustible mystery of human nature, grasped here below only in faith, is this: "The overflow into the creature of that which is born in the bosom and heart of God, an elevation of the creature from its lowliness and separation from God into the bosom and heart of God. Into the bosom of God, so that it is reborn, illuminated by its light, refashioned in its image. Into the heart of God, so that it is quickened by his own Spirit, penetrated by his warmth, fused with him into a single Spirit," as Scheeben says.[2]

The urgent kerygmatic concern of our preaching about the supernatural is that we bring the forever incomprehensible into the lives of the faithful with clarity and ardor and, for that reason, perplexing magnificence of this vocation that exceeds every nature and every beauty of the Spirit. Only in this way

---

[2] *Mysterien des Christentums*, p. 187.

is Christianity clearly understood to be fundamentally the totally other, the unique, and therefore that which raises a claim to be heard with overpowering insistence. Only the message of the supernatural gives the Church and priests the right (all the way down to the last canon of the Code and to the slightest bit of consolation given by the confessor) to come forward with such unheard-of claims. The supernatural is precisely the soul of our kerygmatic, and for this reason every distortion on this point is a sin against the Spirit.

II. THE DOCTRINE OF ORIGINAL JUSTICE AND ORIGINAL SIN

We have already touched upon the original justice of men as it was historically in the doctrine of the supernatural. We must go into it more exactly now, for without the deepened grasp of this mystery it is impossible to preach about original sin and its consequences, hence of the redemption and restoration of the last state.

There comes in addition at this point a matter of great kerygmatic importance. How do we present and preach to the faithful the doctrine about paradise? The way in which we can speak and preach about paradise must give the faithful a deep dogmatic reverence before the mysterious original state of the human race. "Paradise" cannot be for the preacher a word that calls to mind a charming children's idyll, something after the manner of a Rousseauan nature-feeling or the light of a sentimental enthusiasm, as in the text of Haydn's "Creation." It was shown in the eighteenth century precisely on this point that all the "rubbish" about paradise was nothing but a transference of one's dogmatic distortion of the supernatural onto the state of the first man.

It is certain, as our dogma teaches, that with original justice man was given immortality and freedom from suffering. But all these preternatural gifts cannot be understood, not to say tolerated, before we know through divine revelation in what

organic connections they stand. They too had a pure salva-
tion-history significance, and God did not create a pretty
paradise in the first instance for the sake of a pleasurable life
for men, and then all at once, almost from an all too severe
whim, deprive the whole race, for all the millenniums of their
earthly existence, of this idyll. Precisely from the impossibility
of such a representation of paradise can we enter into a kerygmatically meaningful knowledge of this mystery, namely, that
the deepest essence of original justice, and so the state of
sonship with the Trinitarian God (without which state the
preternatural gifts of paradise cannot be organically understood) cannot be clearly known merely from the revelation
of the Old Testament paradise narratives. Only general indications of a one "better" original state can be conjectured
from the darkness of Old Testament revelation. The mystery
of original justice is so great and powerful that we did not
obtain clarity about it before the revelation of the incarnate
Word himself, the revelation of the New Testament. This is true
above all of the deep theology of St. Paul, who is raised
through the divine inspiration of his letters into the bright
realm of infallible divine revelation, and who therefore could
not be opposed to the teaching of Jesus (which confided many
things on this point to the kerygma of the Apostles) in his
theology of original justice—something like rabbinical speculation or dogmatic accretions to the simple synoptic teaching
of Jesus. An enlightening beam from the height of the New
Testament falls back onto the mysterious darkness of human
origins. That is the kerygmatic sense of the basic argument,
familiar to us from Scholastic theology, for the state of divine
sonship in Adam: "Christ restored what Adam lost. But Christ
restored sanctifying grace. Therefore, Adam had sanctifying
grace." We must reconstruct this argument in the simple words
of preaching. We must make the theology of the Epistle to the
Romans our own, and above all appropriate the deep theology
of the early Fathers, principally that of Irenaeus as he expressed it in his work against heresies and (kerygmatically still
more excellent) in his *Epideixis*. Trent preached powerfully

43

in this sense (D. 788): "If anyone does not confess that the first man Adam, through his disobedience to the divine command in paradise, immediately lost that holiness and justice in which he was constituted, let him be anathema."

Our preaching of the beauty of paradise must begin and end with the description of the spiritual, supernatural splendor of sanctifying grace. If we preach this correctly, with God-filled words, we need never draw a distorted and foolish picture of paradise and we can include calmly and with surprising joy the results and conjectures of anthropology about primitive times and the original state of man. For it is precisely in their consistency with these results that the values of the divine economy of salvation shine out all the more. In this economy God elevated the first human couple, at the origin of a cultural development in far distant milleniums, to such a truly and spiritually full supernatural life that there resulted (only now do we understand it correctly and speak of it with organic justification) also freedom from suffering, the integrity of the mastery of the spirit over sensibility (it too willed by God), and finally immortality.

One more word ought to be added at this point in our construction, about the preternatural gifts which were given as consequences, almost as ornaments, along with the heavenly grace of sonship. These graces have belonged since the earliest beginnings of the divine plan of salvation to the full endowment of man, as the Trinitarian God conceived him. In our kerygmatic theology we must never neglect them, even if we do not (as was said above) assign to them the highest importance in our preaching of paradise. This is always allotted to the grace of sonship. We cannot neglect them because they give us the correct and theologically established insight into the correct understanding of the economy of salvation given by the God-man as the second Adam. Even in redemption through Christ the preternatural gifts belong to the full endowment of those to whom the grace of sonship is restored. But they are not given to the individual together with sonship in baptism. They will not be given before the end of human history, when the whole race is fully unfolded from Adam and the prolongation of the race through generation from Adam ceases. Hence they will be given to the completely prepared, existing as one man, Jesus Christ, at the resurrection of the flesh, on the day of the creation of the new and definitive paradise. Further, according to Thomas Aquinas these gifts had to be given along with sonship, for they are organically connected with it.[3] But there exists the marvelous law whereby they return man slowly and with organic growth in the operation of restored grace, in what we call spiritual life. Here in the original history of salvation is the foundation of what we shall later call "holiness" in the ethical sense. The saints, those in whom the grace of sonship in Christ operates most clearly, are those in whom the gift of integrity, the ever more complete mastery of spirit over natural sensibility, more and more break through, in whom impassibility and freedom from suffering come more and more to the fore, insofar as they overcome the deepest of all suffering—senselessness, the state of abandonment to physical and psychic accidents—and are already here below illuminated by a mysterious happiness. Immortality is even now restored to the saints insofar as they are disposed towards the death they must suffer, though in a different way. All of this is so since the second Adam bore the temporary lack of the preternatural gifts in his own earthly life and has thereby elevated and sanctified it, as we will see in our kerygmatic treatment of the life of Christ.

This idea of restoration is our point of departure through which holiness, asceticism, and mysticism become clear in their original theological connections.

Only from a correct understanding of the original state of sonship and its absolute supernaturality can we come to preach correctly about the incomprehensible mystery of our human nature, about the "mystery of iniquity." How far one can go even in our time if he does not clearly see the theological connections of the mystery of original sin, is shown by the

---

[3] See *Summa Theologica*, III, q. 69, a. 3c.

disastrous work, *Der Katholizismus, Sein Stirb und Werde.*[4] It says on page 151: "Whenever a man experiences this mysterious double aspect of sin, this insoluble polarity between freedom and restraint, between guilt and fate within himself, and does not make an accusation against his creator, then he believes in the mystery of original sin, even if he does not also believe in the historicity of the story of the garden of Eden." Here original sin enters into the metaphysical structure of man, "into a pre- and meta-historical" symbol of the universal consciousness of sin. There is no mention of a primitive historical event, still less of what Catholic theology has always considered to be the essence of original sin, namely, the privation of the grace of sonship for the whole race because of a free decision, an historical fact at the beginning of human history. And that is supposed to be, as the book would have it, the deepest meaning of the dogma of original sin. Here it is strikingly clear how far we have gone in these modern efforts to make Catholic dogma current and comprehensible. It becomes just as clear what an urgent obligation we have to preach again today, more earnestly than ever, and with unsurpassable clarity the dogma of original sin expressed by Trent. Original sin is not a symbol for man's universal consciousness of sin, as can be read in the Enlightenment catechisms of the eighteenth century and now most recently in the book mentioned above. Original sin is a mystery of faith which in its essence has nothing to do in the first instance with consciousness of moral life (exactly as in the case of the grace of sonship). Its essence can be grasped only in connection with the historical event in paradise, in connection with the supernatural elevation and the fall of pure spirits, and in connection with the grace of sonship of the first man.

Revelation is always historical, never just a psychological process. Just as we must defend this statement with passionate vigor for Christianity, for the life of Christ, and for the visibility of the Church and the resurrection of the flesh (and so for all

---

[4] G. Mensching, Leipzig, 1939.

that we shall later explain as the visible line of revelation), so must it be done for the beginning of revelation, for original justice and original sin. We must impress again and again on Christians the historicity of the first fall. We use divinely inspired Scripture as our witness. Every evaporation of this process into a mere symbol destroys the foundation of the doctrine of redemption. The life of the second Adam is only as historical as is the deed of the first Adam. What theology calls "the originator of original sin," the free personal act of our first parents, was a unique, historical deed, entered into with full consciousness and clear insight into its essence and its consequences. Today, when we again experience in a living way the fact of human communities and the inevitable consequences that the historical deed of an individual man can have for his whole community, we can again securely presuppose in the faithful an understanding of the sense of the paradise narrative.

It is another question whether the biblical account intends to offer the historical event immediately in the childlike simplicity of the narrative, or if it was intended to be a figurative representation of the historical event after the manner of a parable or a meaningful symbol. We can safely leave this question to the advancing work of dogma and exegesis, taking into account the Church's pronouncements on the matter (D. 2121–2128).

Further, the first sin of man is not to be understood without reference to the mysterious sin of the pure spirits. This segment of revelation, which today goes almost shamefully unmentioned and is sometimes unconsciously avoided, must find here its first foundation in our preaching. For without knowledge in faith and without the correct preaching of this truth (there is also an incorrect way, as will be shown), and so without a mention of the enormous fact that God created a world of wonderful, pure spirits who did not persevere in his grace but plunged into the separation from God that we call hell; without preaching the fact that these fallen spirits entered into a mysterious relation with the first man and that only thus is original sin comprehensible, so that sin propagates itself in mystery from the evil of the fall of the angels down to the last sin of the last man of Adam's race: without all these truths we could never speak correctly about the redemption, about the kingdom of Christ and his victory over Satan, about the grace of baptism as a denial of the devil, about the whole course of history as the slow completion of the expulsion of the princes of this world. Genesis and Apocalypse, beginning and end, the inner finality of the kingdom of God—all are incomprehensible if we do not speak of Satan and his angels right at the beginning of human history in a way that is clear and faithful to the biblical account.

How must this kerygma of Satan be constructed? Here many a pastoral problem lies hidden. Often it seems to be one of the most malicious evils of Satan, who "goes about seeking whom he might devour," that he veils the central truths of Christianity in a cloud of sweetness or (what is worse) in a childishly mystical vapor of dread. This is particularly true of the dogmatic truths about himself. No one likes to talk about the devil. There is, in learned circles especially today, a strong inclination to dispel the biblical doctrine on Satan into a matter of the history of religion, to trace it back to Iranian influences, or to make Satan at least a somewhat nobly sounding personification of evil that is less dangerous than the real Satan. Among the people, on the other hand, Satan is rather a sinister, comical figure, and connected with him are the products of our imagination equipped with horns and tails, the very opposite image to that of the sweet, rosy-red angels with lovely children's faces. In all this the naïvely childlike but still burlesque Middle Ages have deprived the ancient Christian faith even about Satan and his pomp, and of the majesty of this pomp. We must construct, even on the level of the children's catechism, a correct representation of the devil. The inner emotion of the preacher must be continually felt in the sermon, as often as he speaks of this mystery. We will acquire this emotion if we for once earnestly and penetratingly work out our convictions, our words, and our examples from Scripture itself, the Old Testament as well as and especially the New, in which we can experience the enormous drama of the conflict between Christ and Satan, whose force and tension continue in the theology of Paul and in the liturgical language of the Church (baptismal ceremony, blessing of water, benedictions). Here above all we must fashion our kerygmatic language completely and only from the sources of revelation, from John, Paul, and the Apocalypse. "Who commits sin is of the devil" (1 Jn. 3, 8), so much so that Origen[5] speaks correctly of a "mystical body of the devil," since all sins from the very first up until the last judgment are deeply intertwined and the judgment on the devil is extended to all the sins of all men (1 Tim. 3, 6; 2 Pet. 2, 6; Jude 6). The powerful images of Isaiah or the Apocalypse, or a synthesis of all that Jesus said and did against Satan, would result in a full kerygmatic language for a deep and spiritualized preaching of the doctrine of the great enemy of God in this world, without which the drama of the redemption is incomprehensible.

One question which is of primary kerygmatic importance for the total structure of our faith concerns the basic reason for the sin of the angels. Revelation is silent on this point, but it does give us some indications; and from the whole picture of the destiny of the kingdom of God that is revealed to us, deep interpretations can be drawn. We mean the question: Is the sin of the angels to be explained through that trial of faith in which the angels foresaw the future incarnation. It is certain that the inner essence of the sin of the angels consisted in a proud rebellion against the revealing God of faith. According to the teaching of many Fathers and of the theologians who follow Suarez, this pride consisted in a hate-filled rebellion against the incarnation as the middle point of the whole elevation of the creature to a state of sonship. This opinion can be held even if one assumes (as many theologians do) that the incarnation of the Logos was decided upon only subsequent to the foreseen sins of men, and not prior to them, as the

---

5 *Commentarius in Epistulae ad Romanos*, V, n. 9 (*PG* 14, 1046a).

divine-human crowning of the work of elevation to sonship. In this interpretation—namely, that the angels, and at their head the light-bearer Lucifer, that marvelous spirit, refused out of pride to place an act of subordination to the incarnate Logos and rebelled in hatred against this mystery—the parallels between the kingdom of the "mystery of iniquity" and the kingdom of the "mystery of grace" could be shown more purposefully than they otherwise could. It could be shown how the inscrutable hatred of the fallen angels turns mainly (one can say only) against the incarnate God, against the physical and mystical Christ. Jesus himself said with such depth that Satan is a "murderer of men from the very beginning." This means that from the very beginning of sin he thinks about the death of the Incarnate, about the death of God on the cross (the very event by which the prince of darkness is expelled) . . . , about the death of him who is to go forth from the race of Adam. At this point we have insight into how the hatred of the angels penetrates into the destiny of men from paradise on.

We must now show how original sin resulted in a sin inherited by all. Original sin consisted in the privation of the grace of sonship for our first parents, together with the privation of the preternatural gifts resulting from this sonship. The sin was committed with knowledge, enlightened by faith, of the fundamental importance which attached to the first parents as those who, through the sexual activity of generation and birth, were to hand on the grace of sonship to the whole race that was to develop from them, and, indeed, precisely because of this racial unity. They even had knowledge of the fact that God himself would one day assume the flesh of their race. Thus we can understand how immediately after the sin the promise of a woman and her seed was given. Through one born from the seed of Adam all that was consciously squandered for the whole race by the first Adam was to be restored in an enormous conflict against Satan and his seed.

The inherited sin is, therefore, the privation of the grace of sonship freely willed by the first parent and so is a privation that is an aversion from God for the whole race and is thus imputable.

From this clear conception it follows that in original sin there is no question of an essential alteration and deterioration of human nature. In this presentation of the Catholic dogma (with all the differences of opinion as to how far the privation of sonship, for which the nature was destined and created, affected and spoiled this nature), it is possible to confront with true Catholic acknowledgement humanity and its culture, which have not yet come in contact with the grace of redemption, and not to fall into that pessimism of human nature which makes out of genuine Lutheran pessimism (which is related in some way to that of Augustine, as his is to the ancient pessimism stemming from the process of corruption) the native soil for a reaction to the excessive estimation of the goodness of nature, which spread abroad during the Enlightenment and is having its effect even today.

A further result is that the consequences of original sin—man's deprivation of grace and the preternatural gifts—are not only punishment for that unique sin of our first parents[6] but that this sinful absence of grace is a real sin of the whole race. Our preaching must beware of going into the incomprehensible aspects of this mystery in order to make them more plausible. It must be careful of the danger of falling into some form of the Pelagian heresy which saw in original sin only an effect of bad example, and which shifted the whole mystery onto the level of morality, as did Abelard in the early Middle Ages.

Of course, how far our preaching should go into the difficult questions which concern the theological foundation for such a guilt that embraces the whole race is another question. "There is nothing more obscure to the intellect," said Augustine.[7] It is certainly best, if we speak of it at all (and it prepares us for our own theological development) to point to the one great fundamental law which appears also in the divine plan of redemption and restoration. This is the fact that

[6] See the pertinent remarks in Trent (D. 789).
[7] *De Moribus Ecclesiae Catholicae*, I, 22, 40 (*PL* 32, 1328).

51

humanity stands before the eyes of God in the first place as a great unity, and that only in the second place do men stand before him as individuals. We must designate humanity as the one Adam—even though there is in truth no "one Adam" complete in itself—which is now part of the total cosmic process of historical development, and which therefore participates in this totality in grace and in the privation of grace. It is essential for the correct understanding of this mystery (to explain that it is a mystery and can never be completely understood is again and again the task of our kerygma by divine and absolute claim) that we emphasize the fact that there can never be a question of injustice on God's part in the implication of the whole race in the guilt of the first parents, because there is question of the privation of a gift to which nature has no right. It becomes clear at this point that unless we can explain the essence of the supernatural we can never speak correctly of the mystery of original sin. If in spite of all that an unusually depressing element of perplexity about the incomprehensible remains to us, this results from our still not having thought sublimely enough about the inconceivable value of the grace of sonship. And, above all, we have not sufficiently considered the incomprehensibility of God freely and anxiously revealing, whose Spirit "blows where he will," who has spoken in his absolutely free *"placuit."* In this freedom he is incomprehensible. Paul can teach us this deepest human humility in his letter to the Romans. It is a humility which no longer presumes to make only that "entry" from the revealing God which wins agreement from all our petty human calculations.

In the structure of our theology, as it becomes fruitful for the kerygma, this mystery of original justice and original sin, as hardly any other, is suitable to bring out what we have called the invisible line. Not only the grace of sonship, but also its privation for the whole race, give us for the first time a correct insight into the way in which the Trinitarian God wished to communicate his inner life to the creature. But they also show us that we can never confuse (and thereby diminish, almost cheapen) these truly invisible mysteries with

52

conscious elements of the moral life. They show us how these two mysteries live, and live concealed, much more deeply at the root of our soul, and how we can surmise, from the joys of paradise just as much as from the incredible sufferings of fallen humanity, from these visible things as from a distant echo, what took place in us in the realm of invisible things, in the world of divine mysteries which we know from divine and pure faith.

CHAPTER FIVE

THE MYSTERY OF THE HYPOSTATIC UNION

The intimate connections between the dogmatic truths which we have yet to speak of and the mystery of the innocence and fall which we spoke about in the last lecture, is mirrored in the following verse from *The Sibylline Oracles:*

> *The Ruler of the World spoke to his child:*
> *Let us fashion a race, truly mortal,*
> *But which will bear the mark of our own image . . .*
> *And mindful of this decree*
> *The Logos descended to his creation*
> *Clothing himself with his created image,*
> *In a chaste virgin,*
> *Baptizing with water.*[1]

The divine act, ascending from the depths of the freely flowing love of the Trinitarian God, which gave back the life of grace which was lost in original sin, to the race of Adam, which had now become mortal, is the incarnation of God. The Logos descended into a mystical mother, the Church. From now on, the Trinitarian life of the incarnation, his procession from the Father and his possession of his own Spirit, is in an imitative way granted through a virginal, maternal birth, through the Church "baptizing with water." From now on, not only the link of our racial stock with the progenitor of nature, grace—and original sin—is to be determined, but even more our link with the second Adam, the rebirth which takes place by reason of the birth of the New Adam in the Spirit,

[1] VIII, 265–273.

55

is determined. From here on all mysteries, rebirth, the Church, and eternal life are grounded in one central mystery, in the unity of the nature of God and the nature of man in the person of the Logos. Here is the wellspring of the new life in the Spirit, which bubbles up into eternal life, *eis ton patéra*. It is a return to the Father in the Spirit.

God's plan for salvation (be it from the eternal participation of the fall, or before this prescience as the wonderful crowning of all God's works) proceeds towards this one goal, towards the God-man and in him towards mankind who is made "divine" in Christ. Next we come to treat of this grace of Adam, this gift of renewal, "surpassing all our thinking" (Phil. 4, 7), "amplified and more abundant than ever" (Rom. 5, 20; Eph. 1, 8; 1 Tim. 1, 14; Tit. 3, 6). The exuberance and superabundance of this renewal is found precisely in this, that not only do we once more renew the filial grace of our first parents which made them images of God, but we find that the second person of the Godhead has descended into the race of Adam, and that as a result of our blood relationship to him and through the birth from his Spirit of God we participate, in a new way, in this sonship. This union of the Logos with mankind is that "mystery hidden in God since the beginning of time" (Col. 1, 26; Eph. 3, 9; Rom. 16, 25), the sweet mystery—"before the morning star first arose" and "before the mountains came into being"—of his searching love. This love proceeds from the Logos and bursts aglow in his Spirit. Above all else it is the *"placuit"* of his freely chosen personal sacrifice, as the First Vatican Council (D. 1785 and particularly 1789) so wonderfully and understandably recounts. And all the other decrees, even the most puzzling "decrees of his eternal divine will" (1785), are more readily grasped and appear more logical in the light of this decree. They tend towards the Logos, who was made flesh. This is also true of the blessed fault of the original sin and transmitted original sin with its resultant suffering, that is achieved in the centuries of mankind's history. The economy of the Trinitarian God proceeds to the God-man, and from this God-man the world

56

should start to return to a new race. This race ought to proceed from the God-man, from "a man, Jesus Christ," who is himself flesh and blood. Ignatius, the martyr, leaves a comment that reveals the early Christian kerygma in its great depths. This kerygma proceeds from the God-man, and continues to the "new men," to the completed mankind, to the Church, and from there turns home to eternal life.

In a second letter which I intend to write to you, I shall explain more fully what I have merely touched upon, the dispensation of becoming the new man through Jesus Christ, who is of the race of David according to the passion and resurrection. Come together in common, one and all without exception, in charity, in one faith and in one Jesus Christ, who is of the race of David according to the flesh, the Son of man and Son of God, so that with undivided mind you may obey your bishop and priests, and break one bread which is the medicine of immortality and the antidote against death, enabling us to live forever in Jesus Christ.[2]

The mystery of the incarnation of God now reveals itself as the new and the original center of all preaching. It is here that we grasp the very kerygma of God. It must also be the center for our kerygma. Hippolytus of Rome summed it up in the significant statement: "An individual is the child of God. Through God we have grasped the rebirth in the Holy Spirit with the result that it is now our deepest desire that we who are many men become joined with the one new and heavenly man."[3] It was later put into classical form by the great Fathers Athanasius, Gregory of Nazianzus, and Augustine, who initially got it from Irenaeus: the Logos became man in order that mankind become like God in grace. Augustine has treated the relation of the dogma of the incarnation of God with the elevating grace of mankind who had fallen in the wrath of God in the first Adam in his classical kerygmatically accurate writings in the *Enchiridon*.[4]

True to the basic line of progression which we pointed out

[2] *Eph.* 20.
[3] *De Antichristo,* III.
[4] Chapters 10–11 (*PL* 40, 236).

earlier, we ought only to discuss the significance which the "invisible" side of this lofty mystery has for our preaching. Therefore, that which we theologically call the Godhead of Christ must form the focal point of our kerygma even as it forms the focal point for the metaphysical first cause of his place as mediator, of his *gratia capitis*, and of his grace-filled participation in the divine nature which is dispensed through him.

I. THE DIVINITY OF CHRIST
AS THE KERYGMATIC FOCAL POINT

Today, as we all know, this strong link of Christian revelation is being discussed more and more. The complete belief in the true and full divinity of Christ is the touchstone of "positive" Christianity. In the battle over the essence of the freedom of Christian preaching we frequently find ourselves proceeding directly to a historically noteworthy and unnaturally tenacious monotony, when we handle this "sign which will be contradicted" and speak of the divine nature of Christ.

And further: even where one appears to grant the divinity of Christ in order to protect his own religious values, and sees in this reality the link of Christianity, he maintains a peculiar denial against the formularizations which Catholic dogma has given to the truth. Therefore, it seems to be a passing task of our present-day preaching not merely to prove the divinity of Christ in a certain apologetical and fluent form from fundamental theology, but also to protect the metaphysical character in the face of all merely "religious" hollowness, or as it may be better put, to show how the classical definitions of the ecclesiastical teaching authority is not a kind of intellectual "Greek" or "Scholastic" fossilization which disrupts the authority of the lofty mystery, but is born and formed from a religious ardor, which once held the fore prior to the time of the modern and modernistic. It is the spiritual ardor of the Logos whose clarity glows. It alone is catholic, and at the

58

same time it is the Catholic realization of the inner Trinitarian truth that the Spirit proceeds from the Father and the Logos.

How modern man thinks in the area of explanation is best shown in the book which Mensching wrote. In this book "Catholic theologians" present their concepts on the belief in the divinity of Christ. It is presupposed that belief is "the shibboleth of Catholic theology" (p. 134 ff.). But "where this is pronounced with a certain fanaticism, one frequently limits himself by a magisterial formula and so closes the present to many men who are struggling particularly with the access to the ultimate sense of this mystery." "All the terms about the divinity of Christ are human analogies, which are not to be grasped without further ado as the interpretation of a super-natural reality. They have significance in only one direction, not an adequate meaning as far as a total explanation. They ought to serve the fruitfulness of the religious life. Where they can no longer do this, they lose their significance and become merely empty shells and torpid formulas" (p. 135 ff.).

Here the circumstance seems to be radically reversed. It is not true that the religious life fulfills itself and finds its funda-ment in what the wonderful clarity of the thousand-year war of the Church has to say about the divinity of Christ. It is quite the contrary. Held in highest esteem is the pious feeling, the mere similarity with the fathomless depths, which lies hidden in the divine mystery of the person of Jesus. In the course of time this feeling (which is primarily intellect) con-structs forms and formulas which continually turn into hollow shells, if the feeling in its human development has evolved from a protective covering which was woven from the inside out. It is modernism in its purest form, despite the protest which the book makes against such an accusation.[5]

Opposed to that we want to form our kerygma at peace with "fanaticism" regarding the teaching of the Church. Here once again (just as it did earlier in the teaching of the super-natural) the reconstruction of the scientifically theological com-

[5] O. Mauer in his introduction to the booklet *Jesus der Christus,* "Theologie der Zeit," 1936, no. 4.

prehension can never completely dispense with a steady alignment with the scientific itself. Certain dogmatic doctrines have been given ecclesiastical scientific formularizations and then quickly allowed to enter the realm of the boring as "Scholastic formulas." But they have fully entered into the treasure of the teaching Church and so must also be included in our preaching. A man is justified through faith, and faith is called an affirmation of the understanding. This affirmation tends towards the revealed word of God and is only possible in a relationship to a clearly and smoothly molded "word," a "formula." The Catholic belief has never been deluded into believing that the formularizations that have been put forth have exhausted the mystery. But just as "fanatically" must we hold that each doctrinal formularization correctly and accurately expresses the invisibility of the expressed mystery. When in this time the meaningful decision "in a mirror and obscurely" is possible, it is fitting that the revealed word of God be taken up and developed under the direction of the Church.

On that account it is our thankless task to set forth this unveiling of the mystery of God in Christ clearly and historically in order that the people might have an enlightened knowledge of it. With all the expositions and spiritual penetrations achieved in the course of the centuries, the mystery has remained eternally the same. It remains just the same as when it came from the mouth of him "who alone is in heaven, the Son of man. He alone has looked on God and is the only begotten Son, who is in the bosom of the Father" (Jn. 3, 13; 1, 18). On this basis alone can we achieve that certainty through which we can preach the whole mystery of Christ. It also helps us to guard against those who point out to the believer the divinity of Christ as "Johannine," as the smooth, "merely human" picture of the "synoptic" exposé, or against those who point out that the belief in the divinity is a "hellenization" of the original Christian message of Jesus. So says that just-mentioned book of the "Catholic theologians" in a rare contradiction of the view which it set forth of the divinity of Christ. The modern exegete has given us the "historic Jesus" as a truly "great feat" (p. 53). The synoptic Jesus is human, down to earth, bound by earth. He is not all knowing but thinks and lives in the conception of his time and his people. He is not almighty, but pleads for help from his heavenly Father. He is not all holy, but explains that only one is good, the one God! He did not identify himself with the Father, but looked at himself as Son and revealer of the Father. He does not say, "I and the Father are one," but "Father, not as I will, but as you will." In this truly meagre presentation which this book has, one hears almost word for word those things which were presented by a half century of Arians. Desolate rationalism, which stems from Syrian Antioch, was presented against the divine mystery of Christ, and so our kerygma achieves a great victory if we imbue our preaching on Christ with those deep thoughts that are presented in the writings of Athanasius and in the extraordinary formularizations of the Church from the *homoousios* of Nicea to the doctrine of the two natures in Chalcedon and in the fine dogmatic letters of Leo. If we err in this regard it should be towards excess.

Our task and challenge is to present the "I believe in his Son our only Lord" in a more vital manner. We must first of all painstakingly extract the written proof for the divinity of Christ, showing particularly his divinity as found in the synoptic gospels. Certainly we must never oversimplify the problems of the synoptic words "Son of God." At the same time we must add something from the "Johannine" texts (Mt. 11, 25-27; Lk. 10, 21 f.) or from the command to the "mission" (Mt. 28, 18 ff.) which is the basic fundament for those prophecies of Jesus which shed light on his own physical sonship. The picture of the Son of God which John gives in his letters and gospel is not a later "overhaul" brought about through the beliefs of the hellenistic community. Nor is it "the formation of a creating Spirit," nor a "valueless source of a very meaningful belief of the early Christianity" (Mensching, p. 53). Rather, it is a single quite exact and distinct extract which is already established in the synoptic writings. Even today these questions are of great importance in our preaching of Christ and are not to be looked upon as something which belongs to the once-upon-a-time school-learning of a Harnack or even a Bretschneider.

Our kerygma must, more than it sometimes seemed, be formed from a deeper knowledge of the patristic Christology. It should no longer be true that we make a note of a few sentences from the theology of the Church Fathers and let it go at that. We must experience the whole of the early Christian enthusiasm for the mystery of God in Jesus. The problem is how to write sermons using the letter of Ignatius, the *Epideixis* of Irenaeus, and the witness of Christ as found in the acts of the real martyrs as well as the early writing of Athanasius "On the Incarnation of the Logos." These are all imbued with the inimitable fragrance of the early Christian love of Jesus. Also, how can one, following the dogmatically historical development (if one knows them and digs them out of the inadequate remembrance of his school days), come to explain to even the simple believer the events of Nicea, or the heroic defense which Athanasius led against the Arians, or Ephesus and Chalcedon? We ought to keep this historical presentation in our kerygma, for revelation is something historical and the whole mystery of Christ only unfolds itself to us in his historical advent. Otherwise our preaching will be something empty and desolate. First of all, history shows the immovable dogmatic reality in the immediately fruitful and blessed reality of its worldly appearance and through that it awakens us daily to the various choices which we must make: "today if you shall have heard his voice."[6] The "today" of this perduring encounter with the "Word" is the Catholic way of looking at it always dependent on the fact of its historicity. So it is that the conciliar "formularizations" concerning the mystery of God in Christ are not a "Scholastic-dogmatic, historical, and in reality foreign theology" (Mensching, p. 54). Rather, they are the valid pronunciations and human grasp of the whole, which will remain until the end of time as the

[6] *Zeitschrift für katholische Theologie*, 50 (1926), pp. 196–219.

undivided, never exhausted mystery that has brought before us the "only begotten Son in the bosom of the Father."

From the outset the preaching of the divinity of Christ must take pains to present clearly a kerygmatic application that is also found in the other mysteries, but which here has special significance. We saw above (and in the second part of this chapter we will speak more precisely about it) that man today is all too readily inclined to emphasize only the "religious" side, the value in life, the immediate "usefulness" of the dogmas. Now the concept of "religious" is quite broad, and if we grasp it correctly it is taken for granted that dogma was only revealed for the sake of this religion and is not something having no relation to it. Only in Catholic circles are the values which the dogmas have for our lives taken in a too restrictive sense, and (as is related in the book by Mensching) in this number are those "theologians" who, in a completely modernistic way, devoid the concept "religious" of any meaning. Because of the limited value which certain dogmas have for our lives, they do away with them or else circumvent them. Or else they speak of the exalted value which these dogmas have for our lives in a rare, voluntaristic, and merely edifying way (and many there are who cannot do enough in the realm of the "objectively" edifying) and do so in order to make the dogmas more plausible. In opposition to this we want to and must in our preaching hold onto the dogmas, from the divinity of Christ to the character of "absoluteness" and the new reality of revelation which, if one so desires, "stands in opposition to all other religions and is a complete break from the merely natural," as Mensching expressed and then rejected (p. 123).

Primarily from the theology of the New Testament and St. Paul we must carefully work out the supernatural character of faith. This is a stirring assent of all men to the revealed mystery of God. It is an inspired and well-grounded assent to the continuing word of God, though primarily it is essentially a spiritually clear affirmation of the human intellect. The fundamental structure of Christian belief is and always will remain "intellectual." Yet it also remains deeply imbedded in the great risk which is love. Faith is continually an affirmation of an intellectual content to that which we call the word of God, to a truth and to a "theory" in the sense of the Church Fathers. If we fail to reiterate this fact in our preaching of the divinity of Christ, and further fail to illumine it by the internal clarity of faith itself, then in the development of Christian belief we are quite apt to fall into error. This is what happens to the "Catholic theologians" in the work previously mentioned. "They believe in the 'divinity of Christ.' This is in the New Testament sense, not the theoretical acceptance of a dogmatic formula, something of a hypostatic union. Rather, they thankfully and obediently accept Christ as the love act of God which has become visible, and whose continuation finds its completion in doing the right thing and having love" (p. 131). Here, too, in the face of the loud "religious eternal value," the depths of the Christian mysteries and with them the absoluteness of Christian beliefs evaporate. The unconditional totally obedient to the revealing God, taking no account (first of all) of himself; an immediate bare assent to the truth, to the formula which was irrevocably bound with the purely spiritual truth and which certainly not only "means" but is—as far as this is possible—"in a mirror and obscurely," these are also dispersed. According to this affirmation will we be judged, and whoever does not believe will be damned! The anathema of Nicea and Chalcedon is only the wonderful echo of the word of God. The faith is and remains a dogmatic word. That is what we impart to the faithful from our kerygma and our priestly awareness of the sending.

II. THE DIVINITY OF CHRIST AS THE FOUNDATION FOR THE ROLE OF CHRIST AS DISPENSER OF GRACES

Now first of all as we proceed from the holy waste of the unlimited affirmation of faith to the divinity of Christ, we are really able to grasp the value that this mystery has for our lives and at the same time see the warmth of its love. We no longer approach the mystery with the primary attitude that we will merely investigate Christ's relation to us. Because we believe in the absoluteness and importance which this fundamental and proper affirmation has for the creation, we have "leaped into" the majestic task of continuing the revelation of God. First of all, we lift up our eyes so that this self-abandonment becomes a finding of self. We have fallen into the abyss of our own blessedness.

With the assent to the metaphysical sonship of Jesus, the man, we have reached the life-giving focal point from which the sources must now be tapped. The first thing that we must do is try to grasp the meaning of our being Christians. When this is done our kerygma can then participate in the "fullness of the divinity which dwells in him." As now the divinity of Christ is the focal point of the whole cosmos of the economy of grace, it ought also be the focal point for the internal structuring of our preaching. We must achieve this through the kerygma of the divine revelation, and above all through the Christology of St. Paul and the Church Fathers. For as Christ wanted to give himself as God, and only as God, we must preach him as God.

It is now a historical reality of great import that there has been a radical change in the way that the divinity of Christ is preached. The dogmatic conviction has not been touched in any way. Rather, it is the way that the dogmatic data are tied together and preached by J. A. Jungmann. In his work *The Place of Christ in Liturgical Prayer,* he brings this idea out quite well, as is also true in *Die Frohbotschaft und unsere Glaubensverkündigung*, where we find the following basic section: "The doctrine of grace in the apostolic belief in faith and catechetics."[7] Due to the attack that Arianism made on the revealed and—in the early times of Christianity—rigidly adhered to and carefully pondered teaching on the divinity of

---

[7] P. 67.

Christ, great emphasis was placed on the fact of the divinity. The result was that in their kerygma the relationship which this outline had with Paul and the Fathers of the early Church was almost entirely overlooked. The heresy which showed how Christ became God had to be highlighted. From this came the danger that Christ would no longer be presented as the bringer of salvation, but that he would be presented to a certain extent as being empty handed so that people saw in him only the appearance of God, the visible, who has come into the world in order to receive our homage, or perhaps in order to instruct us through word and example. One does not pray any longer so much "through Christ" the mediator to the Father but "to Christ, God." Church and grace are much more readily conceived as the effected work of the Trinitarian God, in whose inaccessible light the God-man as the second person appeared to advance. Here lie the roots for the direction which prayer took in the Eastern piety, to pray to Christ. The typical way in the non-Roman liturgies (the French and Mozarabic, which grew from the bottom up and from which the last hot war against the Arians was led, is to pray to Christ as our God. One need merely refer to the daily prime to find the prayer stemming from the French: "Direct and sanctify . . . Saviour of the world." Here are also found the piety for Jesus which was so prevalent in the Middle Ages. It concerned itself almost exclusively with the love fostered interest in the deep authenticity which comprises the humanity of Jesus who is worthy of our love. So it was that they came to speak of the "Body of God," the "Corpse of God," and this was carried on to the notion of the "loving Father of heaven in the tabernacle." Even today one can find such references in very pious books.

Opposed to this notion the Roman liturgy contained (as Jungmann shows) the treasures of the prayer of a time in which the inner relationships of the early Christian kerygma were still vital. So there grew up in our time, when prayer life and dogmatic thinking are more and more formed in the law of praying of the Church, the desire for a preaching of Christ in the way that it was preached in the kerygma of revelation and the early Church. That is not a revival of the ancient pristine forms, not "an early Christian" playing of games (although they may frequently be played with), but the "today" of the lasting and timeless coming of the Word of God. Even today we can say, "Do not harden your hearts"! Our kerygmatic structure and restructuring must handle that which deals with the divinity of Christ, not so much following the path of the anti-Arian movement, nor even the patterns of the Eastern Christology (which people today prize as a continuing form of the Christology of the early Church, which it certainly is not), but rather the divinity of Christ ought to be viewed as it was contained in the structure of the apostolic symbols and in the sources of revelation, in Scripture, and in Tradition.

In a word, the fundamental thoughts that the early Church held in her preaching of Christ are as follows: the Logos became man, not so much in order to receive the adoration which we owe him, who is of the same essence as the Father (the trembling *proskenesis,* the veiled *leiturgia,* of which the Byzantine *kontakien* and hymns speak so joyfully) but rather, that through him each life becomes transformed in the Holy Trinity, which was lavished upon us when we became members of the race of Adam, and finds its fulfillment in the return to the Father through Christ, who is the source of life. It is Christ who is joined to humanity *"eis ton patéra"* in the Spirit of the Anointed.

Jesus is the man, God, in order that his brothers might become deified. That implies two relationships: the divinity of Christ is the invisible mysterious shimmering fundament for his role as mediator which comes through the visibility of his human presence and so, therefore, that relationship with which he transposes humanity in the Father, "at the right hand of the Father," "always interceding for us." And further: the divinity of Christ is the prototype and basic reason for the manner and way that we received the previously mentioned dispensing of the new life, which proceeds from and returns to the Father. It is also the way that we achieve the sonship of grace, as the completion of the metaphysical sonship of the Logos. The divine birth of grace is the fulfillment of the special way to the Logos, the participation in the divine nature, and the spiritual fulfillment of this "spiritual life" both of the Church and the individual soul. It is the fruit of this completion, this birth from the Father, the communal love in God, and the breathing forth of the Spirit. Only in the mystery of the divinity of Christ does one find the key for the whole and entire understanding of his mediatorship and at the same time the Trinitarian structure of our individual sanctification.

Using this approach to the dogmas, J. A. Jungmann treats[8] one difficulty which remains, namely, that the emphasis of the mystery of the Trinity in the baroque period, in the individual Mass of the Trinity, and in the special "devotion" to the individual divine persons, is nothing more than a somewhat expanded approach to the inner kerygmatic relationships insofar as they are solutions to the previously mentioned and limited anti-Arian aspects. He says, "Certainly the inner life of the triune God is the deepest and ultimate theme of all theology and so at some future time it will comprise the present of our beatitude in heaven. It is taken in this sense in the formula for baptism, at the time when we enter into our life of grace. . . . But here, *in statu viae,* the mystery is really revealed primarily as the pre-note to the doctrine of the Saviour." That is entirely correct. What we mean is that it does not involve "fluent" rearrangement, but that in general the Trinity and the incarnation hang together so essentially that even *in statu patriae* we will not have a (so to speak) purely Trinitarian view of God, but—even through the incarnation of God—in an eternally perduring mediatorship, the flesh of Christ is inseparably bound to the Logos as it enters into the depths of the Trinity. "The mystery of the incarnation cannot be explicitly believed without the faith of the Trinity: because the mystery of the incarnation of Christ does not contain the fact that the Son

[8] *Ibid.,* p. 73. See Jungmann, *Christus als Mittelpunkt religiöser Erziehung,* Freiburg, 1939.

of God shall have taken on flesh and the fact that he shall have renovated the world through the grace of the Holy Spirit," says Thomas.[9]

The opposite is also true in our preaching in this world. We must first of all speak of the Holy Trinity (as it proceeds according to the structure we have established). We have to show that we become worthy of this unheard-of joint knowledge because we ought to participate in this life through grace. So then, e converso we participate in grace because only in this way are we able to "support" the knowledge of this mystery. We hardly should hold two forms of the kerygmatic theology, namely, a Trinitarian and a more Christological. There is only one and that is the wonderful admixture of these two mysteries as Thomas mentioned in the previously cited article. The reconstruction in our kerygma must proceed from that which is first and last in the creed and in the formula for baptism and in every liturgical prayer. We must proceed from the most Holy Trinity, which we only attain "through Christ our Lord." Once we have established this Trinitarian base, then it can certainly be urgent and at the same time "more psychological" to speak more about the way that we can participate in the divine nature, about Christ the mediator, and about Christ the dispenser of grace. But mediatorship and the essence of grace can only be fully grasped as a consequence of the internal divine Trinitarian life.

It is incontestable that the revelation about the incarnation of God both in the Old and New Testaments places the emphasis on the role of intercessor which belongs to the Logos. The divinity of Christ is clearly expressed in the New Testament, in Jesus' own witness to himself, in the Pauline theology, and in the piety of the early community of the Acts of the Apostles. It is just as clear that one does not place the main kerygmatic emphasis on it, but on (without the physical sonship to the Father it is certainly unthinkable) his role as mediator between humanity and the Father. This man Jesus, as the Son of the Father, has in

[9] *Summa Theologica*, II, q. 2, a. 8c.

69

consequence of the fact that he possesses wholly and undividedly the Spirit of the Father, received glorification, the power to stand as mediator between man and the Father. Our own flesh is able to sit on the throne of the Father on equal terms with him. Christ is, primarily, a mediator to the Father, not (as people often say) to "God" in the sense that "God existed before Christ." Nor is he a mediator to himself or to the Holy Spirit, *qua* Holy Spirit. This latter concept, if realized, would destroy the wonderfully delicate emanation of the inner divine metaphysically necessary relations (the divine relations which we once studied with great difficulty, and now show in this valuable and finely drawn inner value which it has for "religiosity"). In our kerygmatic structure it is of prime importance to hear from the very source of revelation the echo of this inner divine relation between the Father and the Son. The divine passion which speaks the human words of the Logos "returns to the Father." It began with the mystery-packed prayer of the incarnation (Heb. 10, 5–7), and continued up till the word with which the human silence of Jesus was, for the first time, broken (Lk. 2, 49), and on up till the last word (Lk. 23, 46), "Abba, Father." That is the pulse beat of his human heart which can only be grasped because we know that this heart belongs to the eternal Logos, who "will forever be born" and who is forever "in the bosom of the Father," even though he came down to us: "without leaving the right hand of the Father."

This outstanding mediatorship to the Father which is found in the person and work of Jesus has been a source of concern for the Arians and the liberal Protestant theologians. Arius and before him Luke of Antioch, Harnack and most recently the "Catholic theologians" of Mensching's book, have quite rightly felt that the most intimate and best things which Jesus revealed to us lie hidden in the kerygma of the Father. "I have told all of you what I have heard from my Father!" But in the depreciation of the mission, whether through the Syrian or modern rationalism, the proper comprehension of these things is undermined. It is more misleading, because of its subtleties, than something which is completely false. It denies that Christ is the mediator to the Father, and relegates the role of mediator to something lustrous but merely temporal. It is this mediatorship (which Athanasius so frequently treated) which primarily bridges the unending abyss between the invisible Father and mankind.

The way that the early Christian community and St. Paul preached about Christ must serve as a basis for our preaching. We must learn to present Christ as the mediator between ourselves and the Father, and we must convey to the faithful the notion of this wonderful Trinitarian structure of the revelation of Christ, the prayer to the Father "through the name of the holy servant Jesus" (Acts 4, 30), "who sits at the right hand of God as the Son of man" (Acts 7, 56). We must teach the hardcore theology of the old Roman conclusion for prayers, "through Christ our Lord." We must awaken in the people the theological tact with which we pray to the Father through Christ in the Spirit, and once more—because Christ is God—show the way as he showed it when he said, "Whoever sees me, sees my Father." Certainly we cannot see Jesus without seeing the Father. We cannot know him if we do not know of his birth from the Father and from that his desire to return to the Father. We can quite simply pray to Jesus and in him encounter the Father in our heart. Certainly, independent of our own useful forms and reflections on the piety in our lives, in all our prayers and petitions, it is Trinitarianly necessary to proceed through the mediator, Jesus Christ, the man (1 Tim. 2, 5). Through his human heart he fits into the midst of the Godhead and so alone will be heard by the Father.

Hippolytus of Rome phrased this concept quite ingeniously: "No man can give the Father the eternal kiss, only he alone who is the first born of the virgin."[10] In him, who through the Spirit of the Father has bound and united us to a completely fulfilled man, can we too give the holy kiss to the Father in our prayer, through Christ.

In these last thoughts we find the solution for many difficulties which present themselves to the pastor and which a liturgically

[10] "Segnungen Jakobs," col. 7 (*Theologische Untersuchungen*, 38, 1, p. 18, n. 4 f.).

focused movement places on a reformation of our already approved prayers and devotions. This conscious reformation is proper and even necessary, as we have shown. But in this reformation we ought not lapse into a theology of consciousness which prays about something as "existing," if it is really there. Here we find the unheard-of heights and authority of the revelation about the divinity of the Logos, who became visible in Jesus the man. This life spreads itself to us in an objective consciousness which has its existence entirely in this world. Consequently, the Trinitarian structure is objective (in every adult active), even if we do not "think" about it or consciously strive to bring it into our consciousness. So it is that each prayer, even the simplest unformed one which is full of the enthusiasm of the "Middle Ages," every rosary, every aspiration to the child Jesus, or to the five wounds, is a prayer through Christ to the Father. That is a fact, not a mere velleity, but at the same time it is not a license to avoid any conscious remodelling of the modern-day piety along the lines of our kerygmatic construct. This ought to be said in order to contrast it with a certainly exaggerated intolerance. All which today is hurriedly formed can first of all be judged in the light of the fundament of all Christianity, in the patience and power which alone is inherent in a true life. Jesus, the brother of man, is God, Christ who was anointed with the Spirit of the Father. Therefore, all prayer and sacrifice of Christians who were anointed with Christ, with the Spirit, is a participation in the divinity of the brother of man, and the Father embraces all of us in the first-born because he alone and we in him possess the fragrance of the anointing with the Spirit: "behold the fragrance of my Son just like the fragrance of a beautiful field which the Lord has blessed" (Gen. 27, 27).

We come next to the second thought which our kerygma of the divinity of Christ must form, the eternal and metaphysically necessary way in which the Logos possesses the nature of God and has, as a result of this, immediately become the prototype for the grace-filled reproduction of our participation in the divine nature. The revelation has already entered into the inner-

72

most and formerly mystery-wrapped and hidden heart of God, which has fulfilled itself in birth from all eternity, in order to give us an insight, a joint knowledge in the special and unheard-of sanctification. If Christ were not of the same nature as the Father, then we would not be elevated and our faith would be absurd. In his second speech against the Arians, Athanasius put these thoughts together in the following way: "Christ put on the created and human body in order to renew this creation, to elevate it to the divine in him and so lead all of us to a measure of his likeness in the kingdom of heaven. But if it were just a binding with bare creation and Christ were not the Son of God, man would not be elevated. Mankind would not have moved to the side of the Father if he who took on our body were not the natural and true Word. . . . Yes, mankind would never have been elevated if the nature of the incarnate Word had not stemmed from the Father and if he were not his own and true Word!"[11]

St. Paul rejoices in this kerygmatic way whenever he preaches about this mystery. From the beginning it was hidden but now it lies open. "Before the world began" (Eph. 1, 4) we were chosen in him and destined to be his children. We are "numbered among the beloved" (Eph. 1, 6) because the Father has only one love, the Child of his heart, the Word whom he let his heart pour forth. Now "the holy one of God is revealed" (Col. 1, 26) to those who "possess the Spirit of Christ" (Rom. 8, 9. 14). That is the heart of the whole early Christian kerygma of the Fathers beginning with Ignatius into whom poured the living water which rushed into his very vitals and said "return, return home to the Father" (*Rom.* 7, 2), and continuing till Irenaeus and Hippolytus, to Athanasius and the Cappadocians, till Augustine and Cyril of Alexandria. That is the act, the "religious" meaning of the dogma about the divinity of Christ, that is the "value for eternity"—but in what a different, deeper, and more metaphysical sense than in the sense of the pre-rational emptying wrought by the present-day Arians! Against

[11] *Adversus Arianos Oratione,* 2, n. 70 (*PG* 26, 296).

these corruptors of the mystery of Christ we must arise as new "immortality," as true *Athanasioi,* and we must preach anew as "peacemakers," as Irenaeus did in his *"Adversus Haereses,"* the unheard-of power of the whole mystery! We must preach to the mature and immature, to the Greeks and barbarians, the mystery which was revealed in Christ, the mystery of his human nature, and then show how now his ungraspable sanctification arises from the faithful acceptance of the revelation of the Godhead of Christ.

Only through hard work have we extracted the point of our kerygmatic construct where the invisible eternal life of the Trinitarian God, which joins itself indestructibly in the hypostatic union to a human nature, was formed in the race of Adam. The second person in God took on our flesh. Now God springs over, through Christ our Lord, to the human race. It is not as if this race would have participated in the hypostatic union in the same way that the physical nature of Jesus the man was given. Rather, all mankind became participants in the unbelievable sanctification, or it should have been prepared for the same through the incarnation of God. We ought also be prepared for the participation in the divine nature, and certainly in a way which deserves the nomenclature "sonship," because it forms an image of that unique way through which the Logos possesses the nature of God, through a birth from God.

It now remains for us—where we still have to treat the mystery of the hypostatic union—to speak about the mystery of sanctifying grace. We must be aware of this mystery because it is of the utmost importance for our preaching that we do not remove the mystery of grace from its inner relationship to the mystery of the Trinity, that is, the mystery of the birth of the Logos from the Father as well as the mystery of the spiration of the Spirit from the Father and the Son. It is still incontestable that the gradual explanation of the doctrine on habitual grace arising from its vital connection with its source, the doctrine of the birth of the "child of God" from the eternal Father, have contributed to a unique stultification which today almost overwhelms all preaching of the dogma of sanctifying

74

grace. The dogmatic wording of the doctrine of habitual grace is very clear, holy, and matter of fact in the Scholastics (something different from the mystifying exposé found in the writings of the Lombard), and in Trent with its reference to grace as an inherent quality. When we preached to the faithful in the past we have neglected the heaven storming and Spirit bearing essence of this divine sanctification, namely, that sanctifying grace is a physical accident according to the way of nature. Here we see more distinctly, as is true in our preaching on many other points of our faith, that the school-measured and clear presentation and meaning of the concept is, to be sure, indispensably necessary. But there is still much to be done in the kerygmatic supplementation. Our preaching ought to become more than a merely vernacular translation and watered-down explanation of Scholastic theses for the simple folk.

We will accomplish this supplementation if we more and more profoundly familiarize ourselves with the interrelationships of the dogmatic truths and pray over them. Here we might try to show this interrelationship in the case of the mystery of our own participation in the divine nature. The mystery of our birth in grace proceeds from the mystery of the birth in God, and barring this fact nothing can be understood. Therefore, the thrilling and joyful fulfillment of the individual sanctification can only be shown when we have first taken a look into the depths of the birth of the Logos from the Father.

The lofty theology of the Johannine prologue announces that the Logos is God. But the Logos was made flesh in order to make men sons of God: "He gave them the power to become sons of God." Only in the revelation of the inner divine Trinitarian mystery can we see this truth with certainty. The total sanctification of the human race in the sonship of God is the main reason why the Trinity, in its love, in the freely flowing *placuit* which was made known in revelation, has revealed the penetrating mystery of its *Trinitarian essence*. Or, in order to speak in the terms of the Church Fathers, this theology (that is, the knowledge of the innermost nature of God) has its one and only inner significance in the *oikonomia* (that is, in the grace-

75

filled decree of God, which lets mankind participate in this life). That is the fundamental thought of the letters to the Ephesians and Colossians. For Paul the incarnation is the focal point for the mystery of God which was hidden from the beginning but is now revealed. That is so because now we were "chosen" in him before the creation of the world" (Eph. 1, 4) and because now "all is bound together both in heaven and on earth" (1, 10). All the centuries pointed towards Christ. And after the Logos took on a human life, birth, and redemptive death on the cross, "the fulfillment of the times" (Eph. 1, 10) and the "end of the centuries" have come over us (1 Cor. 10, 11). From that time on nothing basically new appears. The end of the times is there. There remains for us only the revelation of those things which already are (1 Jn. 3, 2; Rom. 8, 18; Col. 3, 4).

Doubtlessly, that was a fundamental ideal of the early Christian kerygma of grace. God became man in order to elevate mankind. That is the basic structure of the preaching of grace as far back as Ignatius. It was stated with unsurpassable beauty by Irenaeus and Athanasius and with profound and precise control of thought by Cyril of Alexandria. This division of the total accomplishment of all the divine arrangements of salvation, this enormous history of theology whose focal point is the incarnation of the Logos towards which the thousands of years before Christ made pilgrimage, and from which the thousands of years after Christ wander towards glorification—this was the ultimate reason of all Christendom as far as the most spiritual of the Christian heroes were concerned. The incarnation of the Logos is the reason for the significance of all historical occurrences because it gathers together, working backward to the salvific sanctification of the first parents, and forward to the whole of the human race now grasping and remodelling the birth of grace until the resurrection of the flesh, the beginning and end of the history of humanity. "God descended to man and man ascends to God." That was the prime principle for the Greek theology and the mysticism which came out of it. As an heir to this kerygma of the Greek theology of the Fathers, the great Maximus the Confessor presented this primary principle in his work,

76

and the man who knows him best, J. Bach,[12] bound his doctrine together in these words: "The world has to realize a double process, the process of the incarnation which was established from the beginning and has historically realized itself in all time. Then, too, this process of man becoming God finds its fundament in the act of God becoming man. They take place in a parallel way. Each man realizes this most important good, the *Theosis,* only insofar as the process of *Sarkosis* has already begun in him. That is, insofar as he is a living member of Christ and really, through a Christian life, participates in the life and death community of Christ. In this sense, Maximus theologizes not merely from a historical non-recurring event, but also from a permanent, ever present event, the incarnation of Christ in time. Salvation is for him continuing sacramental process of divinization or the process of the ethical spiritualization of humanity which comes from being born of the flesh."

This truly historical concept of the birth of the Logos from the Father and the Virgin, in their relation to our spiritual birth in grace, also became the preoccupying idea of the theology and preaching of the Middle Ages. The ancient mystical cry which was spoken as early as Origen, "What good does it do me that the Logos descended into this world if he is not born in me?"[13] recurs in Augustine and then with wonderful force in the German mystics Eckhart and Tauler. "If that birth does not appear in me, what good does it do me? But that it does appear in me, that means everything to me," says Eckhart.[14] So they have divided all appearances in the universe into three periods which correspond to the three births of the Logos, the eternal, the temporal, and the spiritual birth.

Thomas, too, in his theology sees quite completely the relationship of the incarnation and grace. Precisely in regards to this question in the *Summa* we hear, with particular clarity, the echo of the kerygmatic rejoicing of the Church Fathers. In that

[12] *Dogmengeschichte des Mittelalters,* I, Wien, 1873, p. 17.

[13] *In Jeremiam Homiliae,* 9, n. 1; *In Lucam Homiliae 22.*

[14] F. Pfeiffer, *Deutsche Mystiker des 14. Jahrhunderts,* II, Stuttgart, 1857, p. 3, n. 6 ff.

wonderful article[15] where he speaks about the motive for the incarnation and the explanation which is totally imbued with Augustinian ardor, he rejoices in the same way as the treasured words of Pope St. Leo in the office for Christmas. "Beware, oh Christians, of your dignity, and become consorts of the divine nature. Do not return to your old illness by degenerate talk."[16] Or one can compare that short proemium to the third part of the *Summa* which tersely, but in words filled with wisdom, presents the entire construct with which we here concern ourselves. It speaks of the incarnation as the beginning of man's deification through the sacraments, and the resurrection and immortality as the fulfillment of this life. These notions are also found in the whole arrangement of the forth book of the *Summa Contra Gentiles.*

We must become more and more vitally aware of these relationships. Then our kerygma of Christ will come immediately to the joyous mission of grace and to a lively continuation of the ancient things which Thomas took from Augustine and the Greek Fathers. As he quoted from Augustine: "God was made man so that man might become like God." Then is our kerygma of Christ really a "joyous mission" which is filled with the Spirit and deep thoughts. Thus we obtain that wonderfully virile and yet deeply emotional and dogmatically rich definition which is free from all mere piety. This is found in the text of the Christmas liturgy: "He who was born this day as man was also God. May our gift which is earthly bestow upon us that which is divine."

God was born, the Logos from the Father and the man from the Virgin, so that we might have this sonship. Therefore, that means that we possess this sonship through a way which is similar to the eternal birth. Ours is a birth which is the image of the eternal birth of the Logos from the Father and the birth from the Virgin Mother.

We close this all too brief presentation of the kerygmatic side of the incarnation with the words with which Hilary correlated

[15] *Summa Theologica*, III, q. 1, a. 2c.
[16] *Sermo,* 21, 3 (*PL* 54, 192).

78

the Latin inheritance of the Greek kerygma, the mysteries of the incarnation and grace, and so lead into that which we must handle in the following chapter. "If God grasps us through the human nature because we were far from his nature, in that when he became man he became what we are, so now it is our lot to grasp what he is, to die in order that in our loving haste we penetrate glory . . . and so we grasp that in which we are grasped, in which we acquire the nature of God because God previously acquired the human nature."[17]

[17] *Tractatus super Psalmos,* 2, 47 (*PL* 9, 290a).

CHAPTER SIX

THE PERFECTION OF THE INVISIBLE IN CHURCH, GRACE, AND VISION

In this chapter we shall gather together what has been revealed concerning the continuation and completion of that "invisible line" which proceeds from the Father and which, in Christ the man, passes over to Adam's progeny and leads it in the Spirit back to the Father. In order to bring the Trinitarian aspect of our development more sharply into focus, we might well give this chapter a one-word title: *Pneuma,* Spirit. The way in which the divine life is transferred from the hypostatic union to mankind is typified by the second procession in God, the breathing forth of the Spirit. It is a sonship in love, a coming to birth of the Spirit, a community of all men in the Church which herself lives from and in the Spirit, a continuously operating glorification and spiritualization of the human race under the power of the "spiritual" life even until the resurrection of the body which will be spiritual and, therefore, glorified (1 Cor. 15, 42 ff.). Church, grace, and the beatific vision of God: these are the effects of the Spirit. This is also the understanding of the ancient Christian kerygma, the Apostles' Creed. "I believe in the Holy Spirit": that means "I believe in the holy Church, the remission of sins, and the resurrection of the flesh." We must now speak of these three salvific effects of the Spirit in order to find the correct kerygmatic position for the dogmatic truths of Church, grace, and beatific vision. But before we do that, it is necessary first of all to clarify the vital and organic unity of the teachings of the holy and sanctifying Spirit with the mystery of the incarnation. It is precisely in this point, obviously, that we may

81

in no way alter or omit any of the wonderfully articulated aspects of the interior divine relationships. The *filioque* of the procession of the Spirit is now reflected in the entire scope of the redemptive act. In our preaching we must always be aware of the divine truth that the Spirit is "the Spirit of the Son" (Rom. 8, 9; Gal. 4, 6) and therefore a "Spirit of adoption as sons" (Rom. 8, 14. 16; Gal. 5, 18), and that this Spirit leads us homewards to the Father. From this point of view, the redemptive act of the God-man will become more understandable for us. And so we will speak first of Christ as the giver of the Spirit. Just as Christ poured forth the Holy Spirit by reason of the glorification which he won by his redemptive death and through the participation of his body in the ever approaching *doxa* of his divine nature, so now he can pour out the Spirit upon all mankind. From that point of view the nature of the Church, grace, and beatific vision will become reasonable for us.

I. CHRIST AS GIVER
OF THE SPIRIT TO THE CHURCH

With this plan of incorporating the redemptive action of the God-man into the Trinitarian structure of the entire economy, into that sphere which we are calling "Spirit," we are touching upon a thought that was basic in the kerygmatic structure of the ancient Christian preaching. The great gift which redemption has brought us, the "new life" in the Pauline sense, the "external life" in the Johannine theology, the "kingdom of heaven" in the synoptic preaching: all that is ultimately the spiritual life, the *Pneuma*. And so that which in our previous chapters we have been calling the "invisible line," we now specify here in its passing from the God-man to mankind as the Holy Spirit. We do not so term it insofar as this Spirit is, so to speak, merely a personification of the revealing and redeeming God, but rather in this sense, namely, that the third person in God, the Spirit, Love, Inspiration, Joy, is imparted as an uncreated gift to mankind through participation in Christ. This third person in God

82

wants to reveal himself primarily in such a way that he is revealed in his role of uniting, bestowing, and summoning homewards: in uniting, that is the Church; in bestowing, that is grace; in summoning homewards, that is beatific vision: the Church, the remission of sins, the resurrection of the flesh.

By the words "Holy Spirit" our kerygma of the Apostles' Creed specifies the third person in God, but only insofar as he is a gift, insofar as from him all else develops. In his mysterious parental watchfulness, as it were in his protective lap, there comes to life and is constantly being produced that which is always Life, ever since the moment when this parental Spirit overshadowed a maiden, and when he "brooded over the waters" (Gen. 1, 2). From this maiden, from these waters, there now comes forth the divinely human life of sonship, of participation in the kingdom (Jn. 3, 5).

The bestower of this Spirit (in the full sense of the apostolic kerygma) is Jesus Christ, the God-man. Since his humanity is infinitely holy through his union with the second person of the divinity, since he is truly anointed with the Holy Spirit (Lk. 4, 18; Heb. 1, 9), since he alone possesses the Spirit in its fullness and without measure (Jn. 3, 34), therefore he alone is the dispenser of this spiritual life to all men. He is the founder and originator of the Church. He is the mediator and the divinely human bestower of all grace and he is the "finisher of our faith" (Heb. 12, 2) in the beatific vision.

The humanity of Jesus was to become a sharer in this Spirit in its full effects only from that moment when the humanity was glorified by the passion and the cross. Glorification, the violent emergence of his increasingly spiritualized humanity from its interior union with the divinity, transfiguration (the transfiguration was merely momentary and immediately taken away), is so closely bound up with the death on the cross and dependent upon it that Jesus can simply call this passion his "glorification." Thus does he view as one the death on the cross and the glorification which results from it both for the Father and for himself (see Jn. 12, 23. 27. 28; 13, 31–32; 21, 19, and Heb. 5, 5). This spiritualization, however, is the work of the Holy Spirit:

83

"He shall enlighten me" (Jn. 16, 14), just as it is also the work
of the Father (Jn. 12, 28; 17, 1. 5), and the result of the glorification of Jesus as the enlightenment of the Father, that is, as the
return of mankind, of those whom "you have given me" (Jn. 17,
6 ff.) to the heart of the Father, to the glory which the Logos had
there before the world was (Jn. 17, 5. 23. 24). Thus Church,
grace, and beatific vision originate in the glorification which the
God-man achieved by his death on the cross.

From this fact we now realize what Christ intended to say in
one of the most sublime moments of his earthly life when on the
great feast day he spoke of the living water which would flow
forth from within him (Jn. 7, 37 ff.). John notes in addition:
"The Spirit had not yet been given, since Jesus had not yet been
glorified" (Jn. 7, 39).

This sublime prophecy about living water which is the Holy
Spirit must be read as follows, according to the correct and
established punctuation in the ancient Christian kerygma:

> On the last, the great day of the feast, Jesus stood and said,
> "Let him who is thirsty come to me,
> and let him drink who believes in me."
> For the Scripture indeed says,
> "Streams of living water
> will flow from within him!"
> He said this, however, of the Spirit whom they who had
>   believed in him were to receive.
> But the Spirit had not yet been given since Jesus had not
>   yet been glorified.[1]

In this interpretation the otherwise unintelligible speech becomes transparently clear. The source of the living water which
is the Holy Spirit is the Saviour himself. From within him, from
his *koilia,* that is (if we insert the Aramaic word for it), from his
"heart" the stream of living water flows, and it is only in this
way that there is fulfilled what the Scripture says and what was
symbolized in the ceremony of fetching water on the great feast
day, namely, that when the Messiah comes in the power of his

[1] *In Jeremiam Homiliae,* 18, n. 9.

anointing by the Spirit, he will bestow the Holy Spirit, the living water (Is. 12, 3; Ez. 47, 1; Zech. 13, 1; 14, 8). Only in this way is the prophecy fulfilled which says that the Messiah, as the second Moses of the chosen people, repeats the tremendous miracle which first took place when Moses drew living water from the rock which he struck. The same is true of the miracle of the manna whose fulfillment Jesus promised in the sixth chapter of John. On both occasions the people say, "This is the prophet, the Messiah" (Jn. 6, 14. 30 ff.; 7, 40–41), because they knew the Messiah would be the type of Moses (Acts 3, 22; 7, 27). And so, just as water was struck from a rock which symbolized the coming Messiah (1 Cor. 10, 4), so also living water is struck from the heart of the true Messiah.

This idea now reveals to us the meaning, in John's profound theology, of the fact that at the moment of the definitive glorification on the cross, immediately after the Savior's death, water and blood flowed from his side (Jn. 19, 34–37). By this miraculous process in the dead body of the Saviour (and John states its truth quite emphatically since he himself saw it and testifies to it), a mysterious sign is given that the one who dies really came "unto water and blood." Only by his bloody death on the cross did he merit and bring us the gift of the Spirit, the living water (1 Jn. 5, 6 ff.). This one who has been "pierced" (Apoc. 1, 7) is truly the eternal Son of God. Because of his Sonship, a life-giving effect is proper even to his dead body since glorification begins at the moment of his death. It is at this point that the prophecy of Zechariah (12, 10) is fulfilled by the pouring out of the Spirit through him "whom they have pierced" (Jn. 19, 37). The prophecy of the Lamb is also fulfilled (Ex. 12, 46) because in the glorified Lord John contemplates the Lamb of God. The Baptist had already spoken (Jn. 1, 29) of Christ's redemptive power. This is the Lamb from whose throne the crystal waters of life flow (Apoc. 7, 17; 22, 1), the Lamb who was "slaughtered" (Apoc. 5, 6).

Thus the Dead One, the Slaughtered One, the Pierced One, the Rock that was struck, in a word the glorified Messiah, has become the fountain of living water. Cross and Spirit, blood and

85

water, suffering and glorification are all interconnected. Surely that is the divine exegesis which the risen Christ, "beginning from Moses and through all the prophets," presented to his disciples as proof of his claim: "Did not the Christ have to suffer thus before entering upon his glory?" (Lk. 24, 26–27).

From the very beginning this Trinitarian basis of the passion and redemption was one of the enduring, basic concepts in the apostolic preaching. The Holy Spirit, the fullness and the embodiment of the total redemption, is given to us by the raised and glorified Messiah. "This Jesus whom you crucified, God has raised up: of this we are all witnesses. Therefore, exalted by the right hand of God, and receiving from the Father the promise of the Holy Spirit, he has poured forth this Spirit" (Acts 2, 32–33). For that reason he is the Messiah, the anointed of the Spirit, because he now pours forth the living water. "God has made both Lord and Christ this Jesus whom you crucified" (Acts 2, 36; 5, 31). The preaching of Paul brings out even more clearly what this pouring out of the Spirit consists in: "Through the bath of regeneration and renewal by the Holy Spirit whom he [the Father] has abundantly poured out upon us through Jesus Christ our Saviour" (Tit. 3, 5 ff.). This man, Jesus of Nazareth, who was anointed by the Spirit (Acts 10, 38), can with the breath of his human mouth breathe forth the redemptive Spirit (Jn. 20, 22). He can pour out the Spirit which forms his Church (Acts 2, 38). In bestowing the Spirit he is an Adam, a founder of a new race of the children of God (1 Cor. 15, 45), and he can bestow upon them a "share in what is imperishable" (1 Cor. 15, 50), "eternal life" (Tit. 3, 7); in brief: Church, grace, and beatific vision. And all of this is because he bestowed living water while shedding his blood, because "through the Holy Spirit he offered himself unblemished unto God" (Heb. 9, 14).

Since this Trinitarian aspect of the redemptive act was so firmly rooted in the apostolic tradition and became the basic framework for the kerygma, it was also vital in the doctrine of the Fathers. We intend to pursue this line by viewing the patristic tradition of Christ as the bestower of the Spirit. We are especially interested because we will thus get a foundation for one of today's pressing needs: to base the devotion to the Sacred Heart in the fullness of dogma and tradition. The Messiah himself clearly proclaimed that "from my heart will flow streams of living water."

To begin with, we have here the origin of the image of Christ as it was conceived in the ancient Church even before the exigencies of the Arian heresy shifted some of its characteristics. This is the way the glorified Christ was imagined by the ancient Christians: the redeemer; the Mosaic leader of the new people; the incarnate rock in the wilderness from which living water flows and from whose source the faithful joyfully draw living water; Christ who permits living water to flow from his heart; the Holy Spirit; the spirit of participation in his Sonship, which Origen calls the "paternal waters." Christ is the great, majestic *Soter* who in the Spirit communicates to men some of his majesty, "in order that they might be where I am," who on the cross gained this power of glorification for the Spirit. Christ is the Good Shepherd, the "great shepherd" (Heb. 13, 20), the "prince of shepherds" (1 Pet. 5, 4), the shepherd of the royal sheep, the shepherd with the great, all-seeing eye who grazes his sheep on mountains and plains (see the Inscription of Abercius) and leads the sheep to the living waters of glory (Apoc. 7, 17), "the God of peace" (Heb. 13, 20) who as the prince of shepherds will soon appear in order to bestow the crown of immortality (1 Pet. 5, 4). And so, everywhere we see Christ the glorified one as the "author of life" (Acts 3, 15), in the very act of giving us the Church, grace, and beatific vision, or, in a single pregnant phrase, Christ as bestower of the Spirit and the living water from his human heart.

We will select only a few citations from the splendid tradition of the Fathers concerning the image of Christ. But even these few will indicate that the ancient Christians knew how to preach these truths in a vital manner. They form quite a contrast to the frequently barren apologetic and dry concepts or formulations mingled with a human sweetness with which the image of Christ is explained today. Let this be said once again: one of the very great challenges of today is that we should learn to form our

87

thought and language, our enthusiasm and our praise of Christ, according to the image of the "second Adam who is a life-giving Spirit" (1 Cor. 15, 45). The ancient Fathers of the Church can show us the way.

As early as the so-called Epistle of Barnabas (the first product of the Alexandrian theology to which we are so indebted), the mysterious relationship between "water and cross" was already being pursued. "Blessed are they who, hoping in the cross, have descended into the water." Grace, Church, and beatific vision are here considered as one: "For the prophet says that the land of Jacob was to be renowned above all other lands (Zeph. 3, 20). That means he is giving glory to the vessel of the Spirit, the body of Christ. The prophet says this because we descend into the water full of sin and corruption, and we come out bearing fruits since we have in our hearts the fear and hope of Jesus in the Spirit. 'And whoever eats of these fruits will live forever.' That means, whoever hears these words and believes them will live forever!"[2] In this context we can now understand why Ignatius of Antioch can speak (in passing in one part of his creed) about Christ who "was born and baptized in order, by his passion, to make the water sacred" (*Eph.* 18, 1). This sacred water is the Spirit who is given in baptism, who comes forth from the cross, and who restores the connection between man and the eternal Father. Thus the splendid word of Ignatius adapts itself to this profound kerygma of Christ the bestower of the Spirit. "My love is crucified. Within me there is no longer a fire which burns in an earthly fashion, but living water which speaks inside of me and says to me in my innermost being: Arise, go home to your Father!" (*Rom.* 7, 2. 3). In this eruption of flaming mysticism of the martyr perhaps we can grasp most directly what we are particularly concerned with here. We have here a dogma which is truly experienced. A kerygmatic man of brilliant endowments is speaking.

Justin the philosopher in the dialogue with Trypho the Jew says that the Christians had become heirs because they were allowed to drink from the living fountain of God. For "even

[2] *Epistle of Barnabas*, col. 11.

though Christ was the first born of all creation, he also became the beginning of a second race. The present race was reborn through him—and indeed, by means of water, faith, and wood, for that belongs to the mystery of the cross."[3] Under the influence of the Spirit, Christians even go to death for their faith, "for the name of the glorious rock which sends forth living water into the hearts of those who, through him, love the Father of the universe. And so those who want to drink the water of life, let them drink it!"[4]

We now come to the theology of Irenaeus who, like Justin, continued the Eastern tradition of Polycarp (and, by the same token, of Ignatius and John). Irenaeus has written abundantly on our topic, but we will choose only one reference which, like a creed, comprehends all the notions and which is one of the most profound descriptions of the "spiritual life." "The Father (from whom creation and the Word proceed) and the Word (which proceeds from the Father) give the spirit to all as the Father wills: for its being, in the case of one who is merely created, and for its state as a child of God, in the case of one who is born of God. This then is the result: God is Father and he is over all, through all, and in all. The Father is over all and is the head of Christ. The Word is through all and is the head of the Church. The Spirit is in all of us and is the living water which the Lord gives to everyone who really believes in him, loves him, and knows that 'there is a Father who is over all and through all and in all.' "[5] This is the Spirit who forms the Church, the gushing fountain of the water of salvation which flows from the body of Christ."[6] The Spirit transforms us all, unites us all just "as water unites the grains of wheat to make delicious bread."[7] Without a doubt, this theology was presented in a similar fashion to the faithful in the living proclamation of the word. This theology can also explain that account in the famed letter from the martyrs of Lyons which provides us with

[3] *Dialogus cum Tryphone,* 138.
[4] *Ibid.,* 114.
[5] *Adversus Haereses,* V, 18, 1.
[6] *Ibid.,* III, 38, 1.
[7] *Ibid.,* III, 18, 1.

a valuable and immediate insight into the thought of the Christians of those days. We are told how the deacon Sanctus, in the midst of all his suffering, remained strong and persevered "because he had been immersed in and made powerful by the heavenly fountain of living water which flows from the heart of Christ."[8] In this passage the presentation is quite clearly the result of the correct understanding of John 7, 37 which says that Christ is the great bestower of the Spirit. Christ from his heart *(nedys* has the same meaning as the Johannine *koilia)* gives the Spirit of glory who is revealed on the cross and in martyrdom. In the work of St. Hippolytus of Rome we meet the same interpretation: "Christ the stream is announced to the world through the four gospels and, flowing over the whole world, he sanctifies all who believe in him, as also the prophet says: streams flow from his body."[9] Concerning those who do not believe, Origen says, "They do not drink from the fountain of their Father, nor from the fountain in the temple which summons them saying that if anyone is thirsty let him come to me and drink . . . the waters of Jesus, the waters of Lebanon, the waters of the Father."[10] The water of the Spirit comes from the bosom of the rock, from the pierced side of the Crucified as it once did from the rock of Moses. "The rock was struck and it yields a fountain of water. The side of the Lord was struck and from the cross he released the streams of the New Testament . . . And if the Lord had not been pierced, if blood and water had not flowed from his side, we would all have had to suffer a constant thirst for the word of God."[11] Even the great inscription of the fifth century on the pillars of the baptistry of the Lateran testifies how vital were these ideas from which, in the early Middle Ages, the first forms of the Sacred Heart devotion were begun: "This is the fount of all life which drenches all the earth and takes its principle from the word of Christ."[12]

[8] Eusebius, *Historica Ecclesia,* V, 1, 22.
[9] *In Danielem,* I, 17.
[10] *In Jeremiam Homiliae,* 18, n. 9.
[11] *In Exodum Homiliae,* 11, n. 2.
[12] E. Diehl, *Inscriptiones Latinae Christianae Veteres,* I, p. 289.

Thus does Christ appear to the eyes of the ancient Church and thus must we learn to know him. The Holy Spirit is his Spirit and by the same token the Spirit of the Father.

We have now come to the point in our kerygmatic structure where we must speak of the Church, grace, and the beatific vision. One of today's most pressing problems is how and in what theological context we are to fashion the teaching about the Church. In scientific theology the entire treatise on the Church has all too frequently been remanded to fundamental theology—a procedure which at one time was unavoidably necessary and in the long run has been substantially justified. Nevertheless, the dogmatic teaching on the mystery of the Church, considered only to the extent that it has been thus far in apologetics, can only be handled in passing. In the proper structure of dogmatic theology there is certainly a place for the mystery of the Church.

In the kerygmatic structure of the Apostles' Creed, ecclesiology still maintains its only possible vital place. Immediately after the avowal of the "Holy Spirit" comes the article about the "Holy Church," and the striking repetition of the adjective "holy" is a profound indication of what this continuation of the divine holiness of the Spirit, whom Christ has bestowed upon us as living water, consists in, namely, that which we can call by one word "Church." Church, therefore, is the embodiment of the salvific will of God, the eternal decree that we have already spoken about in the matter of the incarnation. Clement of Alexandria says to the point: "His decree is the salvation of men and is called Church. He knows whom he has called."[13] It is the "Holy Church" because it is composed of the "holy ones who have been called" (Rom. 1, 7). It is the *ekklesia* because it is the community of those who are called. Clement of Rome summarizes the Trinitarian implications of the nature of the Church as follows: "Have we not one God, and one Christ, and one Spirit of grace who was poured out upon us and one vocation in Christ?" (*1 Cor.* 46, 6).

13 *Paedagogus,* I, 6, 27, 2.

Since the Church is the "life of the Spirit" on earth, it is likewise the continuation of the redemption in Christ, the "glorification" of the redeeming death by crucifixion of the God-man who "sacrificed himself in the Holy Spirit." Vatican I also determines in this sense (where even more so the apologetic truth of the Church is certified and the profound material for a continuation of the teaching lies buried in the schemata) in an amazing sentence the relationship between Church and redemption. "The eternal shepherd and pastor of our souls decreed the foundation of the Holy Church so that saving work of redemption would be rendered lasting" (D. 1821).

In order to preach to the faithful the nature of the Church we must ourselves have first searched into the triple relation of its origin. It should not be true that the fact of Pentecost and the coming of the Spirit strikes us as a notable though not quite explicable appendage to the redemptive act of Christ. But rather we must become more and more aware that the redemptive work of Christ was not fully completed until Pentecost and that everything in the redemptive work of Christ had been pointing to this day. This interpretation we have already seen in our consideration of John 7, 39. This is also the meaning of the farewell address and of the entire Pauline theology of the Spirit. Since that "great and splendid day of the Lord" (Acts 2, 20), the end of times has been present because then, and not until then, and from that time forever the "Spirit" is present.

With these thoughts the preaching about the Church moves directly into an eschatological relationship. The Church truly belongs to "the last things." In our own preaching on the Church we must make ourselves ever more enthusiastic over that eschatological atmosphere which is in both sublime and yet affects us with joy. That is what happened on the birthday of the Church itself, on Pentecost. On that occasion, Beginning and End were viewed as one and were verbally expressed in the dynamic preaching of St. Peter. We have to show that the Church is a great drama which is plunging violently to its climax and salvation. It is the drama of the spiritualization of the world as it continues through the centuries, endlessly patient yet breathtakingly purposeful. But it is a drama which consists in an exclusion, in an horrendous struggle between light and darkness, between Christ and Belial. If we place the mystery of the Church in this context and fill it with a truly Christian (not sectarian) spirit of expectation of the *eschaton,* then we will banish that danger into which our faithful pondering of the Church so often falls and about which Peter warned the faithful in his second epistle when he spoke of those who "consider as a delay" (2 Pet. 3, 9) God's ineffable patience, or even of those who begin to mock at the Christian expectation of the end "since everything has remained as it was from the beginning of creation" (2 Pet. 3, 4). The Church is never merely a leisurely do-it-yourself institution, never merely a form of religion which helps us over the difficulties of our lives on earth, which corresponds to our needs and which, at the end, administers to us the comforts of religion. Church as "decision" can only be preached if we also preach about its beginning (which was at the same time its end) on Pentecost amidst the manifestations of the Spirit. The rejection of Satan and his wiles, which in the ancient Christian preaching possessed a very important meaning, would have to be revivified by us. At the same time we would then have an entirely different theological foundation more capable of incorporating into the Church at the right point the "humanities" which people talk about so much today. For they are only the emerging manifestations of the eschatological truth that the Church is always in crisis, that the Church herself is her own crisis, that in the Church the dichotomy between flesh and spirit is continued and thus our present sensitivity for everything merely human is not only a weakness of faith, but an incipient awareness of the ever more closely approaching decision for the day when there will be only "Spirit."

In our preaching about the Church we must above all present it in context with the procession of the Holy Spirit, that is, in its Trinitarian necessity and in its relation with the Logos who with the Father breathes forth the Spirit and

93

as incarnate, pours out this Spirit in order to draw all things to the Father. We cannot speak with full truth about Pentecost as the beginning of the Church unless we have shown how the Church had already begun in that blessed moment when for the first time body was definitely made "Spirit": in the moment of the incarnation; and then in that moment when "Spirit" existed because Christ was glorified: in the moment of death when water and blood streamed from his heart. The spiritual birth of the Church is therefore founded in the incarnation, is symbolically anticipated in its birth from the wound in the Saviour's side, and is finally revealed to men on Pentecost by an epiphany of the Holy Spirit (which parallels the epiphany of the divinity in the man Jesus). That is the spirit-structure of God's whole economy—incarnation, glorification on the cross, the wind on Pentecost, and, as an eternal result, the Church. On this point read the profound teaching of Leo XIII in *Divinum Illud Munus:* "The Church which had already been conceived was born from the very side of the second Adam as he slept on the cross. On that most illustrious Pentecost he revealed himself to man for the first time and did so in an extraordinary way."

To begin with, then—Church and incarnation. As the Fathers say, the Church in a true sense exists even before there are any believers because she has already been given in the incarnation of God. Christ is the first-born among the brothers (Rom. 8, 29; Col. 1, 15; Apoc. 1, 5). The Church is the mysterious union between God and human nature, so intimate that even conjugal union can only be a copy of it. This marriage union began in the womb of the Virgin because "that which is born of her is from the Holy Spirit" (Mt. 1, 20). Thus the Church arises in "that mysterious secrecy where the marital unity between God and man took its origin."[14] On this fact are based the wondrous relations between Mary and the Church which are so profoundly presented by the Fathers, the ancient liturgies, and the medieval mystics. If our preaching

[14] St. Augustine, *Confessions,* IV, 12.

about the Church came from these considerations, how much more fruitful and joyful it would be!

Second—Church from the heart of Christ. Here we come to a teaching which in the ancient Christian theology of the Church was favored like no other and which elicited from the Fathers the most profound and sublimest thoughts: the birth of the Church from the side of Christ.

This consideration is one which can point not only to the richest and most profound basis in tradition, but it also indicates clearly how from this concept of the Church, so dogmatically rich in its implications, we can explain the joy of the ancient Church which history is so amazed at in those first centuries. For that which was written by the deacon Sanctus is truly valid of the whole ancient Church: "It was made moist and powerful by the streams of living water which flows from the heart of Christ." Joy in the Church is ever present, even today, independently of the dogmatic and mystical depth of our kerygma about the Church. As if in a strangely holy and beautiful echo of this wonderful tradition we pray in the office for the feast of the Sacred Heart: "The Church bound to Christ is born from the pierced heart."

Two basic dogmatic considerations of the ancient kerygma about the Church, which are illuminated by the letters of Paul, merge at this point into one: Christ is the great bestower of the Spirit, of the living water from the split rock of his side. And: Christ is the second, the spiritual Adam from whose side the mother of all living, the spiritual Eve, the Church, is formed. Thus the Trinitarian origin of the Church and her relations to Christ and to the Spirit are viewed in a single sublime image. From the Pauline theology of the second Adam, of the motherhood of the Church and her nuptials with Christ, the Fathers form their ecclesiology which is both ardent and filled with luminous spiritual clarity. Here is not the place to discuss the historical evolution of this theology and the preaching of it, although even in this brief selection it could be shown how tirelessly and how full of mysterious joy for every period of the ancient Church this truth was preached even to the simple people. Even in the works of Tertullian this concept of mother Church is proposed as an ancient tradition. In the letters from the martyrs of Lyons we have the absolutely valid proof for the popularity of this profound love of the Church and its power in forming martyrs. In another piece of writing as well, which originated from popular circles, from the period between Tertullian and Cyprian, an unknown writer says, "Our holy Mount Zion is the holy cross, as had been told by the prophets. The law goes forth from Zion. . . . But the law of the Christians is the cross of Christ, the Son of the living God, for again the prophet says, Your law is in the middle of my body. And when he was pierced 'in the middle of his body' blood and water came forth from the wound in his side and from it he formed the holy Church, and in it this law of his passion was to be kept sacred, since he himself had proclaimed: Whoever is thirsty, let him come to me, and let him drink who believes in me. For streams of living water will go forth from his side!" In pursuing the point, it is surprising how the Fathers in their direct preaching of the faith come repeatedly to this mystery of the Church. For example, Origen in his homilies, the great Chrysostom in his eloquent sermons, Ambrose in his talks on the gospel of Luke, and above all the immortal Augustine to whom we are indebted for the fact that the Middle Ages did not forget the truth. The theologians of the Carolingian period spoke of it, as likewise the great Scholastics. In St. Thomas we read of it. In the Miniatures and the Bibles the Church is presented as being born from Christ's wounded heart. Even in the Council of Vienna the mystery of the birth of mother Church has been expressed in deathless words for the whole Church: "After his spirit departed, his side was pierced by a lance so that from the flowing waves of water and wine the one, immaculate, and holy virgin mother, the Church, the bride of Christ, would be formed as Eve was formed in union with and from the side of the first man as he slept" (D. 480).

From the ancient Church's "heart-theology" concerning the

96

origin of the Church from the wound in Christ's side the early Middle Ages formed its Sacred Heart devotion, as the work of K. Richtstätter clearly indicates. In this fact we meet both an invitation and a reproach, namely, that this devotion, a problem to many and a matter of real kerygmatic concern to all, be filled with that spirit which radiates from this sublime tradition; that we do not let it dry up in a fruitless, merely "pious" devotion; that we impart to it some of the spirit expressed in the schemata of Vatican I from which, we hope, at some time a better defined continuation of the dogma of the Church will proceed, just as the Church brings the dogma close to us in the office for the feast of the Sacred Heart. The most sublime gift of this Heart is "Spirit" and its immediate corollary "Church"; and this profound adherence to the Sacred Heart devotion is the article of the Creed: "I believe in the Holy Spirit and the Holy Church."

From this point on, the doctrine of the Church as the mystical body of Christ can now be more clearly presented. According to Pauline theology the unity of the Church is rooted in the profound relationship between Church and Holy Spirit. "One body and one Spirit" (Eph. 4, 4); "For in one Spirit all of us are baptized into one body" (1 Cor. 12, 13). The union with Christ is "Spirit." Irenaeus says expressly: "The communication of Christ, that is the Holy Spirit."[15] Such thinking is along Pauline lines. If we really want to preach the mystery of the body of Christ with the words of revelation, of the divine kerygma itself (Rom. 12, 4-5; 1 Cor. 12, 4 ff.; Eph. 1, 22: Col. 1, 18; 2, 19), if at the same time we do not want to lose the animation of the inspiration in unimaginative clarity, if we do not want to make the doctrine of the mystical body into an exotic teaching or into a merely reasonable but innocuous figure of speech, then our presentation must proceed from the Holy Spirit who gives this body unity and life and its relationship to Christ. "Just as from dry wheat there can be neither dough nor bread without moisture, so also

---

15 *Adversus Haereses*, III, 38, 1.

many of us could not become one in Christ Jesus without the water which comes from heaven," says Irenaeus.[16]

II. SPIRIT AND GRACE IN THEIR BEGINNING AND THEIR COMPLETION

In the sense of the ancient Christian kerygma our belief in the Holy Spirit means above all: "I believe that the 'Spirit' exists." That is to say: I believe that I am living in that sphere of life, in that blessed age, in that portion of God's salvific arrangement which the glorified Lord Christ merited for us and shared with us when he "poured forth the Spirit." That profession of faith describes this new situation conditioned by the Spirit, Church, or in the fuller form, even "the communion of saints." This latter expression in the patristic interpretation of the Creed, which is also upheld by the *Roman Catechism*, means not only the communion of the holy *ones,* but also first and foremost communion of the holy *things,* or as St. Augustine says: "the communion of the sacraments."[17] Thus we believe that every individual man through faith and participation of this "holy thing" in the Holy Church is himself holy. He is holy in the Pauline sense by reason of that grace which we call "sanctifying" or should better call "holy grace" since it does not *make* us holy but *is* our holiness. With this consideration we are touching upon the point where the life of the Holy Spirit, the life of the glorified Lord, the participation in his sonship, is communicated to us through the maternal mediation of the virgin Church in a miraculous birth. In water and the Spirit man becomes a sharer in the royal right, through a rebirth, through a mysterious return to a mother's womb (Jn. 3, 4. 5), through being snatched up into the depths of God by a "blowing of the Spirit" (Jn. 3, 8; Acts 2, 2): "That is the way with everyone who owes his birth to the Spirit." From the description of sanctifying grace which has already

[16] *Ibid.,* III, 18, 1.
[17] *Sermo,* 214, n. 11 (*PL* 38, 1071).

been given we can see how rich and full our preaching of this mystery can become if we gather together, from all we have already said, the individual points bearing on the conferral of grace on man. In a word: our kerygma of habitual grace must allow the connecting lines to the dogma of the Holy Spirit to become clearer. After all, even in the Creed we call the Spirit vivifying. Then the line to the glorified bestower of the Spirit, the Redeemer and his Heart which pours forth the Spirit, will become more and more clear. Grace will be imbedded in the profound dogmatic truth of the "through Christ our Lord" because we are finally bringing out the depths of our "grace-fullness" in such a way that this water of the Spirit, poured into our hearts by Christ, raises us towards the Father.

That is the nucleus of the rich and profound theology of grace in St. Paul and St. John. "He who is driven by the Spirit is a child of God," and this "Spirit of sonship" calls out in us "Abba, Father!" (Rom. 8, 14. 15). Thus the Trinitarian structure of habitual grace is expressed in a wonderfully pertinent way. It immediately follows from this view of grace that it assimilates us to the events of the life which the incarnate One took upon himself (from his birth in the power of the Spirit to the sacrifice on the cross in the Spirit) and by that alone he was transfigured, glorified, and made the bestower of the Spirit. "We must suffer with him in order to be glorified with him" (Rom. 8, 17). "Because you are now sons God sent the Spirit of his Son into our hearts who cries: Abba, Father!"

The Spirit, and likewise sanctifying grace, have only one "call," one *klesis* (and so too the *ekklesia*): Abba, Father. That is his "sight," those are his inexpressible words. The living water in us has only one direction, one thrust: "bubbling up into eternal life" (Jn. 4, 14). But the eternal life is to know the Father whom only the Son knows.

Thus from the nature of sanctifying grace our kerygma is given the possibility of incorporating the ethical, ascetical consequences of revelation with the simple undistorted consequences; from its nature follows the assimilation to the Lord glorified through his passion. There follows the assimilation to his sweet and powerful passion for the Father, this unique, truly holy Spirit of the Sacred Heart devotion. There follows, too, the vital and necessary incorporation of the doctrine of prayer, beginning from the "through Christ our Lord" of the simple prayer to the heights of crucified mysticism which rings in the never sufficiently appreciated word of the martyr Ignatius and was never forgotten in the mysterious history of the mystic souls. In his letter to the Romans (7, 2) Ignatius writes: "My *'eros'* is crucified and there no longer burns in me a fire which is greedy for creatures. But in me is living water which speaks and says within me: Arise, return to your Father!"

In this way, at any rate, our dogmatic understanding and our preaching have found a way of getting out of the unprofitable rut of our preaching on grace. As a consequence of the development of dogma since Pelagius and especially since Baius and Jansenius, it is well known that the speculatively and richly developed doctrine of habitual grace, and the entire grace treatise, have been much too definitively divided from Christology and ecclesiology. If, in opposition, we were to attempt, primarily for our own inner dogmatic thinking and prayer and secondarily for our preaching and catechesis, to let the interrelationships which we previously indicated become known in all their vitality and remain such, we would be avoiding two great dangers. First, we would no longer be speaking in such a way that the faithful almost necessarily formed the notion that sanctifying grace is nothing but a puzzling, almost essential prerequisite, given only once by God, for some vague reason or other, according to his divine pleasure, much as a passport or identification card. Furthermore, we would succeed in making much more vital our preaching about the moral doctrine of Christ, actual grace, the cross, prayer, mortification, the commandments, even heaven and hell, because we would always be connecting up their relationship with the goal which was lovingly established by the powerful triune God with divine passion "before the

100

beginning of time": namely, to bring men home to the Father in the Holy Spirit through the glorified Son of man. Again, in a word: we must present the total teaching of Christian life ever more constantly and clearly in the light of the *eschaton,* under the influence of the final goal.

Thereby we come to the last—and likewise the first. *Telos* and *eschaton* always have these two meanings. They are the end and yet the reorganizing, directive beginning. In Christian preaching eschatology is the most important thing insofar as only from it can the fullness of Christianity be indicated. And thus without this view of the *eschaton* everything falls apart into an infinitely complex, absurdly long, and ever pointless succession of moral prescriptions, testimonials of faith, and good intentions.

It is not as though we were lacking in testimonies of faith concerning the last things. We constantly pray at the end of the Creed "unto life everlasting. Amen." But in preaching, these truths are frequently all too literally the "last" things; just as at the end of a course in dogma, and usually somewhat quickly, we "also dealt with" these dogmas. On this point we especially have need of a reform.

There is a certain tendency among some eschatologists not to acknowledge the reality of the historical kingdom of God on earth and to see in the development of the Church with its concordats, canons, and bureaucracy, simply an "apostasy" from the eschatological teaching of the Church. And therein without a doubt lies a great danger today. Fanatical eschatologists have done even more harm to the kingdom of God than those who have all too easily equipped themselves in the way of the world. But if these "Catholic theologians" see in the second coming of Christ and in the proximity of the kingdom of God only a symbol, a meaningful sign, of the spiritual proximity of the kingdom of God, then they too are basically separating the inseparable unity of the visible and invisible. Indeed, it is true and it is the deepest content of Pauline theology that the kingdom of heaven is already at hand, that the coming *aeon* has already begun, has been in process since the day when "Spirit" was upon the earth. Since the incarnation, since the death on the cross, since Pentecost, the *eschaton* has been present. And if we affirm "I believe in eternal life," then we also affirm not only the belief in the coming *eschaton* but also in that which has come, the mysterious presence of the glorified Christ in the Spirit, in us. But we also joyfully affirm the resurrection of the flesh, and that means us. It means that we are waiting for a termination, for an historical day which is coming. Consequently, it means that we are not affirming merely a symbol but a living, earthly, historical reality. The entire eschatology is Catholic. That is: it is an inseparable togetherness of the other world in this world, of invisible and visible, of heaven and earth, of Spirit and spiritualized flesh.

Our preaching about the last things (to repeat it again) must keep alive in the faithful the living knowledge that Christianity and Church are in truth a drama, an historical process shaped by a tremendous inner dynamism, a conflict between Spirit and Anti-Spirit, between Pneuma and Satan, which begins in paradise and ends on earth when "He will bring to an end all other government, authority, and power, for he must retain the kingdom until he puts all his enemies under his feet and the last enemy to be overthrown will be death" (1 Cor. 15, 24–26). With this knowledge born of faith about the drama of the redemptive act, we banish the great danger which severely threatens our Christianity today, namely, that we degrade it to being "also" a religion, to a shadow of "a natural religion" (with which fundamental theology or theodicy is capable of reckoning but which does not exist in historical reality). We degrade Christianity to a merely consoling function which satisfies our "religious needs" (one of those tricky phrases which bear on their brow their origin from liberalism). We are basically without a goal. We should not deceive ourselves. If not in our attestation of faith, yet certainly in our manner of preaching, our Christianity very often causes a weary, purposeless "this-worldly" impression. Whether we speak about virtue or suffering, the reception of

102

the sacraments or death itself, how often does one get the feeling that all these portions of the Christian revelation and way of life hover, so to speak, in the thin tepid atmosphere of moralizing, separated from all vital dependence on the stimulating truths of eschatology which should awake in us Christians a joy tingling with expectation and at the same time sublime fear. Luke 21, 26 speaks of "swooning with fear." The ancient Christian *Sibylline Oracles* speak of the "world's sweat of anguish."[18] But nevertheless the words of Luke 21, 28 are still true: "look up and raise your heads."

There is still another point to be made concerning eschatological preaching and it is valid even today. We are in the midst of a development in which especially social problems are pressing to the fore. We are in the midst of that peculiar transition period in which the vital, almost nervously keen sensitivity to social obligations, duties, and needs is astir but in which genuine detachment is far from its perfection because real life with its complex historical and human bonds and buffetings flows ever more tenaciously than our spirit which in anticipation hastens ahead of all historically possible development. Consequently, even today the preacher of Christianity is in the awkward situation of standing before men (and himself being one of them) who no longer want to solve their social problems with a few pious platitudes and who yet do not want to throw up their hands in shocking helplessness in the face of current unsolvable problems. Has Christianity failed? Now is the time to re-emphasize more strongly the eschatology of revelation. In defiance of all who reproach us for it, let it once again be called to the attention of the "masses" and affirmed: Christianity is "consolation"; it does not exist primarily to solve social problems. Or better: the Church is the only power on earth which solves such problems because it is the only power which has the courage to say that they are ultimately unsolvable here on earth! With only a Christianity of social progress we limit ourselves understandably but all too

18 VIII, 217.

103

frequently to the level of attempting solutions which are purly "this-wordly." We put aside once again the eschatological concept of man's life until it almost disappears in a "this-worldly" idea. We are not here saying anything against the social ideals and works of today. On the contrary, we are saying something which gives this whole movement inner significance and which truly consoles us whenever all this work seems to be in vain. And so Christianity is a comfort, a consolation, and we should not in shame keep it a secret but we must simply cry it out as once our Lord cried out in the temple (Jn. 7, 37) when he promised the people living water. The socially repressed are thankful for this consolation and are anxious to hear about it. And the socially ideal life on earth would be a shockingly dreadful bit of nonsense without this one idea: the *telos* and *eschaton* of our revelation. That is true first of all in our times when everywhere those organizational forms are smashed without which formerly we could not conceive our Church. It has always been thus in the history of our Church. The fragrance of the Spirit filled the house only after the alabaster was broken (Mk. 14, 3; Jn. 12, 3).

But this fragrance of the Spirit is the sweet expectation of things to come. "You have let fragrance issue forth and I have breathed deeply and now I sigh for you . . . and I am on fire with desire for your peace," says Augustine in an immortal passage from the *Confessions*.[19] This fragrance should permeate our kerygma. We are "spirituals" who must preach the Spirit of solace, and the completion of the Spirit, who has constantly been poured out since Pentecost, is the blessed vision of the eternal, the last day and the beginning of eternity. So it should not be an exegetical riddle for us if, on Pentecost, Peter views as one the Spirit at the beginning and the Spirit at the end. But rather our preaching must be formed on this most ancient of all Christian sermons, the first sermon of the first Pope on the first day of the Church so that we too, inebriated with the Spirit, might come to speak over

[19] X, 27.

and over again of our own most secret longing and that of all Christians, so that we too might be able to speak with a similar wonderful view of all the salvific arrangements of the Trinity: the revelation of the Old Testament up to and including Christ, his passion, resurrection, glorification, his power, his pouring out of the Spirit on all flesh, the Church and her progress towards "the great and wonderful day of the Lord" (Acts 2, 20).

A lot of things still remain to be said especially about the *way* we should speak of the last things, of heaven and hell, of the vision of God and of judgment. But it is even more important that we, in the framework of our Trinitarian concept of God's salvific work, put the last things in their proper relationship with the activity of the Holy Spirit. With irresistible logic, with the logic of the Logos, the Creed has placed the Spirit in context with eternal life: "I believe in the Spirit and in eternal life." For that reason Irenaeus calls the Spirit our "bread of immortality." And in his *Epideixis,* that profound testimony to the ancient Christian kerygma, he summarizes all this in the words, "As Father he is above all; as Word he is with all because all things come into being from the Father through the Word; as Spirit he is in all of us and he calls: Abba, Father, who has formed man in his image. Now the Spirit manifests the Word and therefore the prophets announced the Son of God because the Word causes the Spirit, the breath, to blow, and thus it is the Spirit himself who speaks in the prophets and leads mankind back to the Father. . . . Therefore, at our rebirth baptism is effected by these three. The Father brings about our rebirth through the Son in the Holy Spirit. Those who receive the Holy Spirit and carry him within them will be led to the Word, the Son. The Son in turn takes them to the Father and the Father makes them sharers in immortality. And so without the Spirit no one can see the Word of God, and without the Son no one can come to the Father."[20]

We have traced the invisible line from its origin in the

[20] Nos. 5 and 7.

heart of the Father who bears witness to the Logos, to its return through Jesus, the Christ, in the Spirit to the heart of the Father. "The rivers flow to the place from which they sprang, and then once more flow forth" (Eccl. 1, 7). But we are aware that these streams of living water proceed from the depths of a *man's* heart, and he has said to us: "streams of living water flow from his side" (Jn. 7, 38). They proceed from the heart of a man who is descended from the same proto-parent as we are. This procession and return of the eternal, invisible Spirit-filled life of the Trinity has formed a visible body circumscribed by time and space. It is the body of Christ, born of the Virgin. It is the body of Christ, the Church, which goes down through the ages and returns home to the Father. The invisible has become visible. He who "dwells in an unapproachable light" (1 Tim. 6, 16) is "touched with our hands" (1 Jn. 1, 2). Thus to our kerygma belongs by divine necessity all that we must now develop in the second part of our dogmatic structure: the visible. Therefore, Peter says in the first sermon of the Catholic kerygma: "This Jesus God raised from the dead, . . . and he has received from his Father the promise of the Holy Spirit and has poured out what you see and hear" (Acts 2, 33).

From now on we can see and hear and touch the Spirit: in Christ the man, in the visible Church, in the visible sacrament, and finally, in the resurrection of the body.

106

CHAPTER SEVEN

THE THEOLOGY
OF THE LIFE OF JESUS

"The Word is made flesh." The drama of the divine plan of
salvation does not run its course in the holy, ineffable heights
of pure spirituality which we eye with great longing from
the depths of our disordered entanglement with the flesh. Here
among us and in the very midst of Adam's race, the Logos
has "pitched his tent." Since that time the visible and the
invisible have been indissolubly united. From now on the
divine can only be articulated in human words. From now
on all attempts to gaze upon and to love either the visible
or the invisible exclusively are disastrous and heretical. In
fact, this separation has been a cutting away of the very vitality
of the unity between God and man which has its basis for
all time in the incarnation of the Logos. Consequently, what
the Council of Chalcedon so precisely said of the unity in
Christ also holds true in a very real sense of this union. It
(Christ's nature) is "in two natures, eternally, without any
commingling, or change or division or separation" (D. 148).
The attempt to separate that which is inseparable has always
been heretical.

Thus the theological correctness and fullness of our proclamation is always to be measured by whether or not we are
preachers of this unity of the divine and human and whether
we are catholic in the sense that we surmise and accurately
preach the wondrously balanced mean between the visible
and invisible without the visible becoming wretched earthly
chatter (Ignatius of Antioch would say *"phone"* rather than

107

"logos," Rom 2, 1), and without condemning the invisible to the realm of an intoxicating and ever-empty delusion.

We shall begin, therefore, at this point, further to develop this "visible line" of divine revelation. We will map our course along the guiding lines of the invisible, and, of course according to the order given us in the Apostles' Creed. We begin with the theology of the earthly visible life of Jesus, whose historical tangibility is the prime source for the wonderful tangibility of the invisible divine activity on this earth. Indeed, this life of Jesus is also the very beginning which extends over and beyond itself back to the origins of mankind. The very historicity of the original state of man and of original sin—the "cool of the evening paradise" (Gen. 3, 8), and the apple of sin which "was beautiful to the eye and attractive to look upon" (Gen. 3, 6)—and the historicity of the teaching about Christ in the history of the Jewish people, are understandable only because they have reference to the incarnation of the Logos. From the very beginning this historicity points to the fundamental desire of the Trinity to reveal itself out of love and to communicate this divinely spiritual and invisible Life in an incarnation of the divine, from "the breathing of the breath of life" (Gen. 2, 7) to the resurrection of the flesh in the power of the Holy Spirit (Rom. 8, 11).

Just as the invisible is communicated to us in the kerygmatic structure of revelation in the line: Father-Christ-Church as mystical body-grace-beatific vision, so now the visible as "temporalized" is joined in the line: the earthly life of Jesus—the Church as a visible organization—the sacraments as the sensible means of grace—bodily resurrection. To make clearer the importance of this total view of dogma in the visibility and perceptibility of the God-man and in order to show that in the most recent theological currents there are several ideas circulating whose fallacies can only be known through painstaking study, we must show how, from the beginning of Christianity, the principal source of heresies always lay in the fact that they destroyed the wonderfully balanced unity and hypostatic structure of the dogma on the God-man through an exaggerated "spirituality." In Christianity, by reason of a genuinely Greek (this holds also for the ancient Church) or a genuinely rationalistic (this holds true for modern times) prejudice for the so-called "purely spiritual," everything in human history was seen as a symbol, as an allegory of the incomprehensible, as a pedagogy for the spiritually weaker and for the "mere believers." People saw in the historical reality of Christianity merely the point of departure, the fact to be surpassed, a point of departure, so to speak, for impetuous pneumatomachists. The earthly, the comprehensible, and the perceptible were only the wrappings which the divine naked spirit had to lay aside. The history of these spiritual heresies shows, however, that with the surrender of the corporeal the spirit itself disappeared. Therein lies the most amazing proof for the structure of the mystery of the God-man of Christianity and of God's plan for human nature which was created with a view to supernatural elevation. The Trinity can only be discovered and embraced in the incarnation, which we "touch with our hands." Whoever seeks God apart from this Man will only grasp the emptiness of his own spiritual structure.

This was the monstrous danger involved in Gnosticism from the very beginning. For the sake of a pure spirituality, "untarnished" by the earthly, the earthly form of Jesus was condemned to a mere appearance. The final result was that spirituality was lost with a final culmination in a hideous moral licentiousness. Ignatius of Antioch said, "Some Godless men maintain that Jesus' sufferings were an illusion because they themselves were only illusions" (*Trall.* 10).

If the hellenistic Gnostics did not reduce the body of Jesus to a mere illusion, they did enshroud him with a spiritualized beauty and a blazing light, indicating that they (as Celsus says expressly in his "True Word") consider the merely tangible corporeality of the historical Jesus and his bloody redeeming death as unworthy of the divinity. John wrote an Epistle against all these exaggerations of the pneumatomachists, proclaiming his message from the Logos whom he touched with his hands

109

and who came not only in the water of the Spirit but also in blood, in the blood of his living vital corporeality which was to be sacrificed to death. Ignatius the Martyr and Irenaeus of Lyons wrote against these pneumatomachists. They became the great theologians of the humanity of the divine, which the theologians of the school of Alexandria, beginning with Origen, did not adhere to any more accurately than did the theologians of Asia Minor such as Tertullian and Hippolytus, whose school Rome has always faithfully defended. The rare and penetrating viewpoint of the first Fathers of the Church concerning the earthly figure of Jesus is rooted in this passionate repudiation of all apparent etherealization of Jesus' life which is really the elimination of the human (and, therefore, always of the divine itself). Jesus was not "beauteous," not spiritually transfigured and overpowering conceptually in the sense which the opponent of the Christians, Celsus, in his "True Word" demanded of a God who appeared among men. The corporeal figure of Jesus was insignificant and trivial. The confirmation for this fact was taken from the prophet Isaiah (53, 2). Justin and Clement of Alexandria, Origen and Cyril of Alexandria—who is, frankly, too subtle and too dialectic in his formulations—give expression to this point of view. In a moving outburst Tertullian says, "No matter what his body was whereby men formed their opinions or gazed upon him, whether it was ordinary or insignificant or lacking in dignity, he will nevertheless be my Christ."[1] The genuinely hellenistic spirit which "pneumaticized" the corporeal grew rapidly anew into the heresy of Monophysitism. Yet the bearers of this heresy were the Eastern monks who, under the all too influential Neo-Platonism, and by reason of their mysticism and aversion to matter, lost all sympathy for the corporeality of the redeemer Jesus, of the "man, Jesus Christ" (1 Tim. 2, 5). Because of their theology, the earthly life of Jesus played at first no mediatory role in the mysticism of the Eastern monks, and

[1] *Adversus Marcionem*, III, 17.

110

because they sought to unite this life immediately with the ineffable Father under the impetus of their Gnosticism, this earthly flesh had to be gradually absorbed and swallowed up by the divinity. In opposition to them, Leo the Great, in his immortal *Epistola Dogmatica,* presented the mystery of the visible: "the invisible is born to us in his visible form": "the flesh" is not "absorbed by the divine dignity" (D. 144). The Pseudo-Areopagite drew his writings from his Monophysite spirit in which the earthly is too much refined by the super-divine. Oddly enough, Western mysticism had to endure this for a long time while the Eastern mysticism of Byzantium and Russia today still contain within themselves the dangerous legacy of this onesidedness.

To be sure, the historic greatness of a Basil or a Benedict lies not only in the fact that they had a noble upbringing, and in the case of Benedict Roman moderation, but also above all because from their instinct for Christian perfection they filled the asceticism and ultimately the dogmatic spirit of their monks with the complete doctrine of the God-man. This is quite perceptible in Basil's fight against Apollinarianism, a preliminary stage for the Monophysites. For Benedict and his sons the danger of too much spiritual subtlety in their Christology was always blocked by a pneumatic temporal-mindedness embodied in all its purity in their rule and in the ideal of an order which always stood firmly on earth, yet projected up to the very heavens themselves.

The medieval Beghards are filled with the old spirit of exaggerated spirituality. They "consider it an imperfection to descend from the delicate spirituality and heights of contemplation to the consideration of the Eucharist or the suffering humanity of Christ" (D. 478). And does not a similar danger (even though the last word has not yet been spoken) flash across the lofty heavens of Eckhartian mysticism? Or is this not basically the danger in any mysticism? The great Teresa has depicted for us the significance of this problem in her courageous journey to the Carmel of contemplation. The *Exer-*

111

cises of St. Ignatius can be understood as an historical turning point. Within the concealed and enclosed center of the Christian, and in the spirituality resulting from contemplating the "mysteries" of the life of Jesus, there is awakened the perception for the totality, for the human concomitant state of holy mistrust towards everything exaggerated and enormously one-sided. This perception is significant for the preservation of the totally catholic in the external realm of the dogmatic, too, both in its greatness and in its danger (for everything great is dangerous), whether this great danger and dangerous greatness be the heroic spirituality or worldly renouncement of the pneumatomachists of all ages, or the quiet modesty and the sober orthodoxy of the "psychists" whose modesty easily becomes lifeless virtue. Ingatius does not have us contemplate the "mysteries" of the life of Jesus for no reason at all. His *Exercises* are by no means only a praiseworthy, almost playful, or purely historical occupation with the life of Jesus in Palestine, nor piously edifying literature on the life of Jesus in the sense of the rationalists from Pelagius down to the contemporary. Rather, they establish for a moment that wonderfully balanced medium between flesh and spirit which is still preserved by the best of his sons and spiritual heirs. Many who appealed to him sank too frequently into the earthiness of mere edification, and others who opposed him by reason of an exaggerated spirituality and "pure prayer" lapsed into a still more fundamentally desolate pneumatomachy (from which even Bremond is not to be absolved). The solution is articulated neither in spirituality nor dogma, but rather in the mystery of the life of Jesus, in the *Exercises,* and especially in the liturgy, in which the ancient and balanced wisdom of the Church teaches us to read and contemplate each day the deep mystery of the life of Jesus.

We now find ourselves in the midst of the question towards which our inquiry is directed. History itself has lead us into it. It remains now to show how we ought to consider and proclaim the earthly life of Jesus.

112

I. THE THEOLOGY OF THE LIFE OF JESUS

First of all, we must say at the very beginning that such a theology does exist. Precisely because we are always not only historically but also psychologically in danger of separating the spiritual and other-worldly from the earthly, the earthly life of Jesus has descended to a mere historicity, to an exegetical compilation of the facts of his life preserved in the gospels. These facts are the object of our belief (*per accidens*, as it were) that he is God. The life of Jesus for us is fragmented into pericopes from which we derive edifying examples for our need and consolation—the object of our imitation. This is all good. But the mystery of this life is still untouched. We must to some extent say *a priori* that obviously the earthly life which the Logos himself condescended to lead in a highly delimited area of our history was replete with divine mystery and wonder in every single instant. All of this "signified" something in the profound sense of the word, it *points to*, it is the clue to something greater than itself, it is the sign of something invisible, it lives between spirit and flesh at every moment, in every action and in every word. We might bring this notion directly into the sphere of allegorical exegesis just as Origen has left it behind for us as a dangerous inheritance to the truth. We banish the danger of any pneumatic onesidedness with the constant acknowledgement of the earthly, historical comprehension of this life by saying in the Creed: "under Pontius Pilate," by letting nothing in this life evaporate into mere symbol.

There is nothing in the life of Christ which is not of unending value to us, starting with his swaddling clothes (Lk. 2, 7) up to the vinegar of his sufferings (Mt. 27, 48) and the folded linen cloths of his resurrection (Jn. 20, 7). These are all *semeia*, signs penetrating as it were the veils under which we sense his *doxa*. They are the epiphanies of his glory in the

113

sense of Johannine Christology (see Jn. 1, 14; 2, 11), but nevertheless they are also the earthly, conceptual, singular, historical veil in the land of Judah of that time and by the banks of Genesareth. Because everything is disguised, everything remains in the merely earthly sphere for him who sees not with the eyes of faith. The life of Jesus is a single, large parable which was spoken "in order that they might see and still not see, hear and still not hear" (Mt. 13, 13; Mk. 4, 11). "The humanity or rather the human nature of Jesus was certainly visible to the natural eye of man. But the divine dignity and personality of this Son of man, the hypostatic union of his human nature with the person of the Son of God, the fullness of divine being dwelling in him and the streaming richness of the divine splendor and sanctity, were concealed from earthly eyes and from all created reason. The visible humanity of Christ, visible in its natural constitution, . . . was subsumed into the unapproachable light of the divinity, in whose embrace it rested and which filled it with glory. We are not saying that the humanity of Christ in itself was a mystery. It was visible. It bore this mystery in itself and concealed it through its natural visibility; for while Christ was found to be exteriorly like other men, at the very least it could be learned that he was interiorly more and infinitely more than "mere man."

However, since we now know through faith the hidden divinity of this man, the task of the theology of the life of Jesus consists in this, that we "see, hear, and understand" (Mt. 13, 17) with the "blessed eyes" which see what kings and prophets did not see and so beg that our eyes be not "held" when the humble Jesus breaks the bread before our eyes (Lk. 24, 16). For just this temporality of God is the only way to ascend to the "gnosis" of his splendor. The Church so passionately professes his corporeality in connection with the "epiphany" and the "becoming transparent" of his *Doxa* that the proclamation of his flesh is never absorbed into the proclamation of his glory. "In the truth of our flesh he appears visibly as corporeal": thus proclaims the canon of the Epiphany because only in the creedal embrace of the visible "are we able to be transported to the love of the invisible."

With this introduction we must now approach the contemplation of the mysteries of the visible life.

From this point on we shall first of all establish the correct theological standpoint (and such today is terribly important) vis-à-vis the plan of salvation in the Old Testament. We already saw in retrospect that the life of Jesus completely shaped all events from the moment when in the first man rested "the seed" of the human nature chosen out by God. Therefore, the trembling, expectant love of God already spoke at the edge of the lost paradise about this "seed" as though it could not wait to reveal to men the deeply concealed meaningfulness of the now-accomplished world-event which was to reveal itself only after thousands of years. Thus the prophecy was made to Abraham that in his seed all nations are blessed (Gen. 12, 3; Gal. 3, 16). For this reason the dying Jacob prophesies the "ruler from the loins of Judah" (Gen. 49, 10), who at the same time is the "expectancy of the pagans." It is precisely to these marvelous prophecies of our ancestors that the Fathers of the Church, above all Hippolytus of Rome and Ambrose, have applied their profound and rapturous ideas concerning the meaning of those "patriarchal blessings" in an allegory which doubtless is theologically more correct and truer than a merely critically oriented exegesis. Therefore, we must understand the entire Old Testament from the point of view of Christ. The history of this nation, of these people who were permitted to prepare the "flesh" for the Redeemer, is and remains for eternity of thrilling interest for us Christians who offer the "flesh" of this man on our altars and who believe that this "flesh" sits on the throne of God. The history of the people of Israel is the history of Jesus, his family tree, his earthly origin. It is not "merely" a divine plan of salvation, somewhat like a proof for belief in one God, but it is for us a pedagogy directed to Christ in all its manifold characteristics (Gal. 3, 24). Everything in this history is (just as in the life of Jesus itself) full of portents and the strength of parabolic witness. All the

115

events in the history of this nation up to Christ are at the same time a history of salvation, a foreboding of what is to come. The journey through the desert (Jude 5), the serpent on the staff (Jn. 3, 14), the water from the rock (1 Cor. 10, 4), the manna (Jn. 6, 32), Moses the prophet (Acts 3, 23): all of these "took place as a sign for us" (1 Cor. 10, 6), that "the God of Abraham, Isaac, and Jacob has glorified his servant Jesus" (Acts 3, 13). The letter to the Hebrews is an eternally orthodox sign for us that this "allegory" of the Old Testament is proven to be correct. Jesus himself has, "beginning with Moses and all the prophets, explained everything written in the scripture concerning him" (Lk. 24, 27). Thus the Old Testament in its entirety must become for us, too, not just a few singled-out texts which proclaim him who is to come. We must complete the God-man's exegesis which he gave to the disciples on the way to Emmaus. This is the best apology of the Old Testament.

We will now concern ourselves with the *earthly* life of Jesus. Indeed, it has been striking that the inspired witnesses sent by God who have imparted knowledge of this life to us in no way "relate" the life of Jesus as one would ordinarily relate an earthly life from birth to death. The evangelists discriminate. For them this life is an unprecedented drama in which everything, even the minutest detail, is ordered to a climactic goal, to an apocalypse of divine splendor in the redemption, and in the combat with the powers of darkness. Matthew, in his breathtaking insistence on the crisis with the Jews so unworthy of the divine calling; John, with his grace-laden outlook on the divine background of all the earthly activity and suffering of Jesus, both show us that even for us the earthly life of Jesus must be in truth a mystery, the parable of an entire life which is capable of solution and understanding. Therefore, it is our first task, through a penetrating, loving perusal of the gospels, to make this inner purpose of the life of Jesus our own. To put it negatively, we must emerge from this simple, almost naïve presentation, as if the revealing God has related "stories" to us in the inspired gospels, as if he had come to the point of reporting to us the life of Jesus almost to the point of exhaustion. We must discover

116

the profound reason why the gospels ruthlessly suppress everything which seems to "interest" us so vitally (in a theologically
disturbing arrangement): all the events of the childhood history
(which characteristically enough were "enlarged upon" by
apocryphal Gnostic sources), the thirty years at Nazareth, the
precise time of the teaching activity, all the events which according to the conclusion in John could not be contained by all the
books of the world. "There are, however, many other things
that Jesus did" (Jn. 21, 25). Is not this the shuddering, really
exciting fact: God permits that most of his earthly deeds,
beginning with the ordinary things in his daily life up to date of
his birth and death, be forgotten, be argued over, be seemingly
unimportant and insignificant in the streaming light of this one
fact—that he has come to save us, to complete the battle with
Satan, to raise to a newness of life. The word of the apostle is
valid for all ages: "And if we formerly judged Christ according
to the flesh, now we no longer do so" (2 Cor. 5, 16). Regarding
Christ and his earthly life there is no longer a dependence on
the mere things of the flesh. God himself, the inspirer of his own
writings, has forgotten them, as it were. With Christ it is not
like Augustus and the other great men "in the flesh" of whom
we possess exact dates of birth and death, statues almost true
to life, and the true reporting of their deeds on marble. Of Jesus'
earthly form we know nothing, nothing of the writings which he
might have written (not that he did), nothing in the way of
statues or relics. For his earthly life, although still hidden and
still untransparent in the weakness of the flesh, was already a
mystery, already in the realm of spirit. Let it be understood
correctly: we do not wish to speak of an almost Gnostic glorification or "Docetization." For us the earthly life of Jesus remains
that entirely conceivable, singularly historic plan which was
carried out on the streets of Palestine, "in the synagogues, the
villages, and the spots where Christ our Lord preached and
traveled" (Ignatius, *Exercises,* 91). But there is also another
danger which is just as great: that our interest in the life of
Jesus become all too earthly, or as Paul would say, "fleshy."
There is a danger that we fall into that attitude which regrets

117

that we know "so very little" about the life of Jesus; this attitude
feels that such details would signify something of value from the
point of view of the history of salvation. Rather, our theology of
the life of Jesus must be fundamentally rooted in what is guaranteed to us through God's Spirit, and this theology must spring
from what has actually been given.

This theology consists in this (we can at this point give a few
indications), that first of all the life of Jesus in Palestine is the
prototype of the life of man before his God, *the* outward form
of the divine among men. This is so not in the manner of
"transfigured humanity" as the liberal theologians always made
of the life of Jesus, but as the prototype of grace-laden, divinized man whose pardon (as we saw previously) has its ultimate
basis in the hypostatic union of this human nature with the
Logos. But precisely for this reason the earthly life of this man
who is God must, on the other hand, be in all its human aspects
the prototype of the Christian man. Jesus' earthly life is therefore in its totality the prototype of the servant of God, of one
standing before the majesty of God. We ought not let ourselves
forget this profound and austere characterization of Jesus as
pasis Theou, of the servant of God, and how it stands so powerfully represented in Isaiah (42, 1 ff.), and how it is proclaimed
emphatically by Matthew as fulfilled in Jesus (12, 18): "Here
is my servant whom I have selected, my beloved who delights
my heart; I will endow him with my spirit." Thus have the
Christians in the primitive community prayed (Acts 4, 27) concerning the "servant Jesus, the holy one, whom you have
anointed," "through your servant Jesus."[2] The characteristic
pais, puer struck a familiar note in the minds of the earthly
Christians. It carried with it everything which is hidden in the
word "child" relative to childlike love and mysterious intimacy.
In this one word the lofty mystery of the person was expressed
who, since he is the Child of the eternal Father and yet (and
for this reason) the obedient servant of God in his human
nature upon which the Spirit of the Lord has fallen, now drives

[2] *Didache,* 10, 2, 3.

118

forth to obedience unto death in the desert (Mt. 4, 2), and to the cross (Phil. 2, 7; Mt. 20, 27. 28). His earthly life—or better, that which we know of his earthly life from testimony—is therefore the prototype of this complete subjection to the will of the majestic God. But this subjection is a vital submission to the hands of the *Father*. This is the second point which we must infer from his earthly life—the relationship of Jesus to his Father. We already spoke of this matter in connection with the mystery of the triune God. Now at this point we approach from the outside to the inside. We learn of this mystery in the lonely hours of prayer of this man on the dark mountains of Galilee. We experience his inmost love from the stammering words with which he speaks in his own peculiar manner of "his Father." For our theology of the life of Jesus this speaking must not be some sort of accident of synoptic reporting, but an august mystery, since the first human words with which God himself breaks the silence of thousands of years in his incarnate Logos are: "Did you not know that I must be concerned with my Father's business?" (Lk. 2, 49), and the final words that he spoke "in the days of his flesh": "Father, into your hands I commend my spirit" (Lk. 23, 46). In Jesus, who is the Son and at the same time the servant because he is God and man at the same time, the Christian mystery of the natural and supernatural finds its foundation. So, too, his earthly existence becomes more and more the vital, antecedent, ontological prototype of all Christian existence.

The divinely inspired apostles immediately place everything which they report of the life of Jesus into this exalted context. The infancy narratives in Matthew and Luke are not pretty, pastoral additions to Mark, but took their birth from the same spirit of heroic contemplation of the life of Jesus of which Paul spoke: "Born of a woman, born under the law, so that those who were under the law he might redeem" (Gal. 4, 4 ff.). The reports concerning his hours of prayer and his inner struggle with the Father are not given for the sake of moralistic proto-typical edification. These reports have meaning only when we hear them as the manifestations of the depth of his high-priestly,

119

human heart whose mystery we can only intimate from his being deeply rooted in his eternal birth from the Father. This is articulated in the Epistle to the Hebrews, where we see the immediate connection of his divine and human priestly dignity with the *ego hodie genui te:* "Jesus in his life on earth offered prayers and entreaties, crying aloud with tears, to him who was able to save him from death, and because of his piety his prayer was heard. Although he was a Son, he learned to obey through what he suffered" (Heb. 2, 7–8). When we read of the hour of his transfiguration, we must place it in most profound relationship with what the aging Peter spoke of years later (2 Pet. 1, 16–17). His suffering is the great testimony, the martyrdom of Jesus in the real and profound sense (1 Tim. 6, 13) through which he became the "trustworthy witness" (Apoc. 1, 5), through which he "resisted sin unto death" (Heb. 12, 4). With this we come to the principal theological notion which Peter and Paul expressed so often: that the entire life of Jesus (and above all his death) was a singular, continued fight against Satan, the *conflict* of God with the opponent from the very beginning. In this context we must again and again see all the events of the earthly life of Jesus: his preaching of the kingdom of God, his conflict with the demons, his miracles, his temptation, his battle with death in the Garden of Olives, his death on the cross, where he "disarmed the principalities and dominions and displayed them openly, triumphing over them through him" (Col. 2, 15). Finally, there is still another allusion which we spoke of before: the theological meaning of the veneration of the Heart of Jesus, the piercing of the side of Jesus and the flow of blood and water. We must free even this fact from its merely earthly context, as John himself has done so marvelously in his allusions to the Old Testament prototypes, in his Apocalypse where he speaks of him "coming on the clouds and every eye will see him, even the men who pierced him" (1, 7); and as he does in his epistles when he tells of him who "has come in water and blood" (1 Jn. 5, 6).

Therefore, to take up again the terminology of our introductory remarks, we must ever allow the "visible line" of the

120

earthly life of Jesus to be embraced, as it were, by the mysteries of the "invisible." We must view both together as one. The life of Jesus in Palestine must become for us the "epiphany" of the divine splendor, not an edifying, narrative succession of the God-man events. The unfolding of the earthly life of God must be a history of the divine. Only in this manner will we become men who love the invisible because of our recognition of God in his visibility.

The life of Jesus in its completely singular, concrete historicity, which as such cannot be repeated, which took shape under completely determined, historical, social, and geographical circumstances, is therefore the prototype for our Christian lives. But this is not primarily in the traditional sense of "imitation," but in the sacramental, theological sense of the mystery of the body of Christ continuing in Christians whose destiny is prefigured in a mysterious manner in the earthly life of Jesus himself. Only this aspect of ontological prefiguration of the Christian life (and, of course, with so much the greater impetus) makes moral imitation both necessary and possible. This is the theology of *syn,* of life "with Christ." The Christian life is, in the depths of its spiritual structure, a recapitulation of the earthly life of Jesus (which always concealed what was spiritual). Grace is a being born from God, a being with the Son, a being crucified with him, a rising with him, a sitting together with him on the throne of the Father (Rom. 6, 6; Gal. 5, 24; Rom. 6, 4. 8; Col. 2, 12; 2 Cor. 7, 3; 2 Tim. 2, 11; Eph. 2, 6; Col. 3, 4; only to name a few words, for this theology is not "constituted" in a few citations but belongs to the foundation of the entire revelation in the New Testament). Christ is in us (Col. 1, 27; Eph. 3, 17). Christ is growing in us from the beginning (Gal. 4, 19) on up to maturity (Eph. 4, 13) and "the making of our poor bodies over to resemble his glorious body" (Phil. 3, 21). The earthly life of Jesus in its entirety has become the fundamental basis for our life of grace: this is the theological background for the fact that always in all Catholic asceticism which is attuned to the God-man the imitation of Christ is the essence of spirituality. Thus Ignatius in the *Exercises,* has us contemplate these mysteries

121

because in their course from Christ's birth till his death on the cross from which glory increased, they are the development of that which Ignatius said at the beginning of these contemplations: "Whoever desires to come with me must labor with me so that, following me in labor, he may also follow me into glory" (*Exercises,* 95). This is true not only (if one is permitted to speak in such a manner) for the original facts in the life of the God-man, for the birth, death, and resurrection, but also for the entire succession of events in his life and for the circumstances of this earthly existence. Nevertheless, in our most profound moments this must be a problem for us: why God in the form of man came into the world as he did and not otherwise—from the Jewish nation, of a virgin, as a poor man, hidden for thirty years, his activity confined to just this small nation, dying such a death. Why all this? Surely it was to show in a vital manner the basic structure of everything Christian: that Christianity is simply *the* renunciation of the "world," the great sign of contradiction to everything which appears to us rational, natural, and plausible; that in the obtuse and narrow-minded way that we possess the revelation of God, we ourselves threaten to lose the sense for this unheard-of "irrationality" in the life of Jesus; that Christianity nevertheless in its depths is basically poverty, chastity, and obedience. Christianity without the glory of the cross is a nonentity and therefore a scandal to the Jews and Greeks. These events also point out that within Christianity the mysterious ascents of the spiritual life cling to the prototype of the earthly life of Jesus in the wandering from the peace of Nazareth to the noise of the three years of preaching, from the transfiguration to the cross: "Let no one say anything concerning this vision until the Son of man has risen from the dead" (Mt. 17, 9). St. Ignatius with a marvelous discernment of the relationships between the decisive texts in his "Second Week" has set up meditations on Jesus in the temple: "Did you not know that I must be about my Father's business?" (Lk. 2, 49), and Jesus in the desert: "Let it be so this time for it is right that it be fulfilled by us" (Mt. 3, 15). Christianity in the full sense of the word is "decision"—thus Ignatius wishes his

122

Exercises to be understood—and to be surely an assent to the Father in a "no" to everything human in the maternal Nazareth.

The experience of Jesus in the temple and his going into the desert are mysteriously repeated in the life of Jesus here on earth or elsewhere where in a mystical crisis everything is detached from the soul which is not "God all in all." Everything which was in the life of Jesus is repeated in the life of the Christian: the weeping and jubilation, the thirst and the hunger, the anxiety and the joy, the marriage feast and the plucking of corn, hosanna and crucifixion, the passion with its temple and veil split (Heb. 10, 20), the suffering beyond the city gate (Heb. 13, 13). Everything is the *kenosis* (emptying) of the genuine Christian from whom the glory of the God-man breaks forth, for "our life is hidden with Christ in God," because "we are dead" (Col. 3, 3).

From this sacramental foundation of Christianity as an ontological imitation of the earthly life of Jesus, it follows that the morally conscious, systematic contemplation of the *Imitation of Christ* (which people brush aside so willingly and so unjustifiably with a gesture of contempt as "moralistic"—as if there existed in Christianity something "only" moral and as if there were something ontic that had no effect on our acts)—must belong to the essential elements of Christian piety. It may be that many representatives of this modern devotion, the simple, pious, heartfelt contemplatives of the life of Jesus, have not been clearly conscious of the theological foundations for their piety. They approach from outside in, they glance back at the earthly life of Jesus as on something past, as a life of the saint which they believe is the most beautiful and most imitatable life of all, as though they were contemplating and imitating the life of the dear mother of God. It may be that "classically formed" Christianity is not always lived out. But it is precisely here that a great mystery of Christianity reveals itself and becomes the most comprehensible element in the theology of the earthly life of Jesus. Christian devotion is not dependent on the awareness of those who are Christians; it is not a "gnosis" which is only reserved to the pneumato-

123

machists and closed off to the "many." Christendom possesses the metaphysical accuracy of Love, and this is often more vital in those who approach the inner truth from the outside simply and in a childlike manner, who with their rosary and their not very liturgical attitude, are much more profoundly involved in their faith than those who make the quality of their Christian-being always dependent on their reflection. The martyr Ignatius knew this truth and expressed it when he wrote to the Romans (3, 2–3); "Beg for me the strength both interiorly and exteriorly not only to *speak* but to *will,* that I be not *called* a Christian but *prove myself* to be a Christian. Nothing is good which is visible here below. For our God Jesus Christ appears much more resplendent now that he is again with the Father. Christianity is not the work of persuasion, but of inner greatness as long as it is hated by the world."

This is the most profound meaning of the life of Jesus—and at the same time the deepest apology for simple devotion to Jesus, because in Christianity everything which happens in grace shares in the glory of him who is no longer visible because he is with the Father, because he is hidden in God and because from now on only this is true: "When, however, Christ, our life, appears, you too will be made resplendent in glory with him" (Col. 3, 4).

II. THE PREACHING OF THE LIFE OF JESUS

How must our Christian kerygma now take shape on the basis of the view we have elaborated above? Basically, there is one thing first of all: our preaching of Christ must remain alive to everything that is visible and invisible in the mystery of Christ. We may not debase the life of Jesus into a biography, not even the great mystery of Nazareth, not even Bethlehem. Recently, there has been frequent and just opposition to certain infantilism not only in art but even in Jesus-spirituality. It may seem as though we had laid a foundation in what we said before which renders this sentimental and childish lack of reverence not only emotionally or artistically but (what people scarcely sought to prove up till now) even theologically unacceptable. But—and this is important—we acquire from this theology of the life of Jesus also that serenity which does not reject everything which people nowadays like to characterize in their immature zeal as sentimental or childish. There is also a genuine childlikeness, and some people remain children always and require something childlike throughout their lives. There are also today too many Gnostics who, out of an exaggerated spirituality, wish to take away from people the rather earthly atmosphere in which alone their pious and simple love can live. Why are we so afraid that the childlike beginnings to our attitude on faith might harm and narrow our great faith? The soul of man is still close to God, the creator, when it constructs its world in the realm of creation. Even the great, the mighty, the supernatural needs the natural and the earthy in which it can take root and grow strong. The earth is varied and good, and everything that she lets live and grow is constructed according to the pattern of the distant one on high who ineffably dwells in us. We must not "heavenize" the life of Jesus. That would be just as false as if we were to look on it only in an earthly manner. Even the Risen One ate roasted fish and honey (Lk. 24, 42). "A spirit does not have flesh and limbs as you see in me" (Lk. 24, 39). The precious care in Jesus' earthly life for the everyday, his understanding of and participation in the trivial which is such a part of human life, is continued without interruption (but transfigured by the impatient smiles of the spiritualized man) in the days following his resurrection when he stood on the shore of the lake and stirred the coals on the fire (Jn. 21, 9). This is our Master! Thus we must proclaim him! We must oppose the Gnostics of our day with the immortal words of Ignatius the martyr when he appealed to the Christians: "Close your ears as soon as someone brings you teaching without Jesus, the Christ, who took his origin from Mary, who was truly given birth, who ate and drank, who was really condemned under Pontius Pilate and died, who also really rose from the dead when his Father awakened him" (*Trall.* 9, 1–2). Our proclamation of Christ

125

must leave room for simple, popular, traditional piety. It must, in a word, be and remain "Logos in the flesh." For again Ignatius says (*Eph.* 8, 2): "Even what you do according to the flesh is spiritual, for you do everything in Jesus Christ."

On the basis of the theological insight which we gained in the first part into the meaning of the particular facts and circumstances of God's communication to us of the earthly life of the Logos, we will now establish the principle that our kerygma of the life of Jesus has to hold completely to that insight and may not "know more" (Rom. 12, 3). This brings about, however, two conclusions: one that we do not wish to "augment" the basic knowledge given through the revelation of the inspired books by going to other sources, above all to any private revelations or to pious contemplations which attempt to offer what is new and hitherto not known.

This principle needs further interpretation. First of all, we have no intention of opposing any scientifically valid exegesis which helps us to extend the historic, cultural, and religious background of the reports of the evangelists, or more precisely to recognize any unanticipated vitality acquired from the holy texts themselves. This would be the case if exegesis, with the help of ancient cultural history, allows us to understand more graphically and therefore more impressively certain events in the life of our Lord. All this, however, is nothing but reverential devotion to the word of God as it now presents itself, and "exegesis" is therefore in the most profound sense the most reverential title for this "ministry of the word" (Acts 6, 4), because exegesis is not arbitrary and artistic embellishment but the *unfolding* of the word of God. On the other hand, attempts to "fill out" the gospels should be judged in a different manner. The Gnostics have left behind an abundance of apocrypha which were later tirelessly worked over into their catholic meaning to oppose to some degree the childlike, almost touching attempts of simple believers at "innovations" of this type. The Fathers of the Church with their classically formed Christianity, supported by biblical theology, were always wary of these prolific growths of popular love for Jesus. And rightly so. What Paul had said

126

rang in their hearts: we know him no longer according to the flesh. What type of genuine religion could build on this kind of preaching about Jesus? What was the guarantee for all these things which can momentarily have an "edifying" or touching effect, but doubtless lose that abiding strength which belongs alone to the word of God? A filling out of the evangelical reports, therefore, with additions from Anna Katharina Emmerick, for instance, is inadmissible. Something quite different, on the other hand, is a rather hesitant, wise usage of these and similar writings which are accepted patiently by the Church as a substitution, so to speak, for the work of scientific exegesis which we spoke of above. What it comes down to is this: if this application proceeds with theological and religio-psychological tact, if above all the essential difference between holy Scripture and private revelations of this sort is always perceptible to believers, then something from these works of the suffering of the life in Nazareth can be used for devotional revivification.

It is better, however, if the priest always develops in himself a vivid growing sense for the heroic beauty and the luminous purity of the evangelical text (especially if he prays over it). What a difference there is between the noble, tacit reserve of the biblical reports, and the loquaciousness of the apocrypha and private revelations! Our proclamation of Christ must also be full of this disciplined and divine tact.

Further, one of the results of the principle which we have articulated above is that our kerygma must not concern the *object* of evangelical revelation (even if this is developed exegetically in a scientific or popular manner), but also the *kind* of revelation it is. That means that we must work out for ourselves a schema, as it were, of the life of Jesus in which the individual pieces, parables, and instructions have their organic place. We must seek for the meaning behind the mighty drama of the life of Jesus. Then we will be able to offer a new and forceful explanation of the individual pericopes. Is it not true (unfortunately) that there are many priests who gather for themselves some knowledge of the constantly recurring pericopes, but for whom all the other sections remain in a kind of rare

127

semi-darkness? Certainly on Sundays we must and should evaluate homiletically the pericopes proposed by the Church. But does this mean that we may explain only this definite part and not the other pericopes which unfortunately almost always remain untouched? How forceful and often how captivating can that preacher be on the life of Jesus if he really knows it!

Thus we have presented in basic outline a "theology of the visibility" of Jesus' life. The visibility continues now in the Church as the visible, organized mystery comprehensible historically and sensibly in its office, law, and sacraments for all those called to be one people in the Church. Irenaeus of Lyons has grasped the relationship between the visible Christ and the visible Church in a striking phrase: "This predetermined, visible appearance of the Son of God among us, his incarnation and his delay in our midst, when we have previously no knowledge of him, the Word revealed through Isaiah in utterance: 'I became *visible* for those who did not desire me and was found by those who did not look for me. Behold, here I am, I said to a nation which did not know how to call out my name.' "[3]

---

[3] *Epideixes,* col. 92.

CHAPTER EIGHT

THE THEOLOGY
OF THE VISIBLE CHURCH

The prophetic words of Isaiah: "Here I am! Here I am!," were fulfilled in the earthly life of Jesus and continued in history within the Church. The Church, as we have seen, is the continually vital reality of Christ. She is the focal point of the nations which formerly "did not seek God and did not know how to speak his name." Just as Jesus Christ concealed the glory of his divinity within the humility of his earthly form before his resurrection, likewise the Church is not only the mystical body, but also up to that final day the body of humility (Phil. 3, 21). Our preaching of the faith must do justice to this fundamental and often painful reality. There exists also a Docetism and Gnosticism of the body of Christ which is his Church—even now! There are Christians who cannot bear to hear the Church proclaiming unmistakably and clearly to the world, "Here I am." They would prefer to conceive of the Church as some sort of superior, spiritually concealed community, and they would like best of all to characterize everything that is comprehensible about her in earthly terms—the organization, canonical law, central administration, Church policy—as a dangerous pact with the world and as a fleeting concession to human weakness. Sohm's famous antithesis between the Church of love and the juridical Church has been presented so plausibly and with such spiritual erudition by its initiator that it continually finds among its open and secret followers those who have not secured a theological position from which the solution of this great problem can be lucidly balanced.

129

From the fact that the Church of Christ is a vital continuation of this double mystery in Christ, Logos and flesh, visible and invisible, two great dangers have resulted which have been a constant reality in history.

One consists in an excessive spiritualization of the concept of the Church. An example is the poignant and passionate manner in which Tertullian carried on the battle for a purely spiritual Church in his Montanistic writings and for this very reason cut himself off from the visible Church. There was at all times the treasured hope among Christians that the time would come when there would be just "spirit." Therefore, there was at all times the fearful temptation to hasten the coming of this so-called spiritual period, to substitute for the "body of humility" a spiritualizing process that would absorb everything fleshly, and to bear submissively with Christ and the Church in patience until the Lord would come. The Catharists of the Middle Ages and of our own time, Joachim of Fiore and our Adventists, Luther with his spiritual Church and the pneumatomachists of our own day: they all possess a high but ethereal picture of the other-worldly Church and so put aside the flesh of the Church which has formed itself in the patience and divinely willed chance occurrences of two thousand years. The *Una Sancta* movement spearheaded by Friedrich Heiler, the Spiritual Church advocated in most recent times by the "Catholic theologians" in Mensching's book, the countless faithful who in their disillusionment and anxiety are overwhelmed by the human elements of the Church in history and at the present time—all are in need of a true and genuine theology of the *visible*.

This theology is just as important for the Church as it is for the life of Jesus. We must incorporate these notions into our preaching about the Church if we want to speak to the men of today. In the Foreword to their book, the "Catholic theologians," in a summons which is difficult to determine as being touching or pathetic, say: "Thus we dedicate our work to all those who believe in the great *Una Sancta* and who fight and suffer for her. Help, brothers, to secure the divine mystery in the face of the meddling intellect, from the onslaught of the juridical and

130

the darkness of magic, so that she will become the torch of the future!" This Foreword strikingly indicates what the contents of the entire book will be. The purely spiritual Church of the body will be finally freed from the intellectualism of dogma, from the juridical elements of law, from the magic of the sacraments. Instead, she will be the "strong spearhead of orthodoxy," and thus separated brethren will note "that everything which separates us is only the work of man." The papacy and its claims to primacy of right is to be led back to the "Tertullian-Syrian" conception of primitive Christianity. The "magic" (apparently the sacraments) is to give way to a spiritualized conception, above all with respect to the Eucharist which has been so annoyingly materialized by Scholastic theology. In a word, the Church must again become what she was before the outbreak of the "canonical" mode of thought. She must become a community of love in the Holy Spirit.

Clearly and unmistakably, there is opposition here to what is called in fundamental theology since the time of Bellarmine the "notes of the visibility of the Church" and the visibility of the Church in her dogmatic avowals, in her law, and in her sacraments.

The second danger which we must also point out is an exaggerated emphasis on this visibility. There are men, even theologians, who (to apply Paul's words here) "only know the Church in the flesh." They value the Church for her two-thousand year history, her amazing organization, her astounding ability to be able to assume the best in surrounding culture and still remain true to herself. They praise the Church as a singular complexity of opposites, as the vital principle which accommodates herself to nations and times without abandoning her essence, and finally as the great pastor of souls down through the centuries. This is all true even if it should be introduced more often with greater caution and historical tact. The visibility of the Church in her amazing expansion (even viewed purely in historical terms), in her fruitfulness generated with almost mysterious power from the times of apparent and real decadence, in her "inexhaustible productivity in all good" of which

Vatican I speaks (D. 1794), is without any doubt an excellent motive for belief and an historically acceptable proof for the fact that divine power must be at work in the deepest essence of the Church and that she is in fact the "signal raised for all nations" (Is. 11, 12). But all of this must not be confused with a short-sighted and precipitous optimism which can still be heard in apologetical defenses of the Church. Such is not the case as though the history of the Church were a continually unfolding process towards a future complete state with the result that the now of the Church contains (almost like the Darwinian conception of evolution) all the accomplishments of the past within her and that the Church progresses from victory to victory and from light to light.

Today when everywhere we find collapse and destruction precisely with respect to that superficial, ecclesiastical, cultural optimism of which we were so proud, things which we have too easily confused with the nature of the Church, or elements which in accord with their ecclesiastical conception belong to the area of the essentials of the Church and to her valid claims, but which the Lord of the Church allows us to misplace—these very elements we ought to recall in a theology of the visible within the Church. We must allow ourselves to be led by the present history of the Church into its own profundities, into the "abyss of the judgment of God" (Ps. 35, 7). The mysterious surrender of the Church to foreign powers and still more to the embarrassing human elements within her own ranks should not drive us in comfortable flight to a purely spiritual Church, nor still less should it back us into a comfortable subterfuge of a "properly adjusted" history of the Church. The history of the Church is and remains like her Master a "sign to be contradicted," a great puzzle, not only a motive of belief but also proof of faith, a divine "temptation"—even up to the very day when "many will fall away because their love has grown cold" (Mt. 24, 10. 12). The end will be "when false Christs will appear to mislead God's chosen people if they can" (Mt. 24, 24). In no way does the history of the visible Church run its course so that belief becomes easier and easier, or more plausible and worthier of men. It is the other way around. At the end of time the Anti-Christ with his signs and wonders and the heroism of his "desert" and the culture of his "comforts" will be the embodiment of everything natural and self-evident. The Church, however, is and grows more and more. The "little flock" (Lk. 12, 32) of which the Venerable Bede speaks (and which we so often read in the office) "wants to increase in humility up to the end."[1] We must accept all that is human and the all too visible element of the Church in this apocalyptic sense. The visible element in the Church which we stare at in our weakness of faith and which perplexes us or is disconcerting for the bride "without flaw or wrinkle" (Eph. 5, 27), must become for us (and to be sure, precisely in this is its healing visibility) "a likeness of the unseen" (Col. 1, 15), just as the man Jesus from David's lineage, from Nazareth "from which nothing good comes" (Jn. 1, 46), is the wretched one, the bloodied figure on the cross, who in redemption is nevertheless the image of the unseen God in whom "everything visible and invisible is created" (Col. 1, 16). We must recognize by faith the divine invisibility in the visible Church. Her humanity must become translucent to us, and, by reason of her poverty, we must be convinced that the Church, because she is the mystical body of Christ, must become necessarily in addition "despised by the people" (Ps. 21, 7), "despised and like one from whom men hide their faces" (Is. 53, 3) and whose form is "beyond that of the sons of men" (Is. 52, 14). The Church is journeying towards the cross. This is what is the most significant of the theology of her visibleness. The powerful words of the Epistle to the Hebrews are applicable to her: "It is faith that enables us to see that the universe was created at the command of God, so that the world we see did not rise out of matter" (Heb. 11, 3).

We must now try to understand this visibility of the Church in a theological context which will help us understand both her dogmatic necessity and religious depths. We must indicate precisely that this visible element is the incarnation of the invisible

---

[1] *In Lucam,* IV, 54.

Church, how it makes perceptible the great call of the imperceptible Logos who calls his Church together, the living body of the great mystery which is present in Christ and the Church. From this it follows that we are never able to love and embrace the spirit, the mystical and invisible in the Church, if we do not love her body. This will be possible for us by a dogmatically correct attitude towards the *entire* Church which is each assent to the spirit and flesh of the Church. In its ecclesiastical context it is called *sentire cum Ecclesia,* and it points out one of the really great fundaments of our present-day preaching.

I. THE VISIBILITY OF THE CHURCH AS THE EXPRESSION OF THE INVISIBLE

Historical, visible and perceptible corporeality belongs to the essence of the Church as long as she is a pilgrim here below. This is true not only in the sense that this visibility is merely the apologetic point of contact for the invisible nature of the Church, and therefore "really" does not belong here (Tertullian would say that this visibility is only for the "psychists" and must be surmounted by the genuine pneumatomachist), but it is also true that we may understand corporeality here and now from the supernatural nature of the Church herself. This we derive first of all from the *name* of the Church as *Ekklesia.* The Church is the union of those "called together" by Christ. Above all we must first work out this dogma of the calling from the theology of St. Paul without which we will not understand the depths of the visibility of the Church. The new economy of salvation brought by Christ is no longer the mere belonging to the race of Adam, but it is the principle of pardon, a call, a choosing, a being set aside. This is certainly not to be understood as irrevocable predestination, but as an action made possible by God himself, in which an accepted or rejected answer to this divine call and submission in faith is given. This mysterious call proceeds from the incomprehensible depths of the divine good pleasure, and the Church takes her very origin

134

from the moment when for the first time a man speaks, the God-man: "I come to do your will" (Heb. 10, 9); and "he called to himself whomsoever he himself wanted" (Mk. 3, 13; Gal. 1, 15). Wherever this divine call comes from the depths of the divine mystery, from the *placuit* of his free election within humanity, he forms for himself a body, the body of the God-man from the Virgin, the body of the Church formed in the calling forth of the apostles, who now continue to carry the call to humanity and thus form the body of the Church, made up of those who teach and those who listen. Paul has articulated this truth in the profoundly significant section in his Epistle to the Romans (8, 29. 30) where the roots of the visible Church are found in the depths of divine predestination. Here too is found the return of this visibility into the hiddenness of the divine countenance: "For those whom he had marked out from the first he predestined to be made like his Son, so that he should be the eldest of many brothers: and those whom he has predestined he called, and those whom he calls he makes upright, and those whom he makes upright he glorifies" (Rom. 8, 29. 30). From the depths of the divine nature comes the call to the visible light which is first manifested in the first-born of the brethern. The one body of these brethren who are called (*kaleo*) together is the Church (*ekklesia*), and it has justification as its single task. This justified "solemn gathering of all God's first-born sons" (Heb. 12, 23) returns to glorification in Christ. Thus the circle is closed. In the Johannine sense: "Father, I wish to have those whom you have given me with me where I am, to see my glory that you have given me, for you loved me before the creation of the world" (Jn. 17, 24). In the marvelous cycle of the divine economy of grace which proceeds from the invisible and returns again to the invisible, there appears for an instant (and this movement we call the history of the Church) the visible in its concrete, bodily form, and it must be assented to and embraced as such by those who wish to be justified. This call is, accordingly, the ever resounding and at the same time body-forming Logos. From the "nothing" of the divine distance he awakens the body of those "who are there" (Rom. 4, 17; 1 Cor.

135

1, 28), the community of those who are named: "People, beloved, children of the living God" (Rom. 9, 24. 26), "saints whom he has called" (Rom. 8, 28). The innermost secret of this calling (and therefore also the community of those who are called, the *ecclesia*) is certainly "unending inheritance" (Heb. 9, 15), "wonderful light" (1 Pet. 2, 9), "community with his own Son" (1 Cor. 1, 9), in a word: the "hope of the calling" (Eph. 4, 4: 1, 18), the call to "glorification and to the kingdom" (1 Thess. 2, 12), to "perfection" (1 Thess. 5, 24). But this mystery of the realized future of the coming age is not an esoteric mystery, not merely lifeless and interior, but a perceptible call, always going forth from the mouth of man until the end of human history. "And how are they to believe him if they have not heard him? And how are they to hear unless someone preaches to them? And how are men to preach unless they are sent to do it?" (Rom. 10, 17).

The Church is, therefore, the continuation of the eternal Word, proceeding from the mouth of the Father, because "their voices have gone all over the earth" (Rom. 10, 18), and now for all times the Word is true: "So faith comes from hearing what is told, and that hearing comes through the message about Christ" (Rom. 10, 17). This signifies the immediate and interior connection between the concept of the "Church" and "apostolate": "hearing, however, through the word of Christ."

The perceptible and ceaseless call to be carried by man presupposes that formation which makes from "nothing" a "people" and the organic distinction between the teachers and listeners, in preaching and obedience. The divine call never goes immediately or in a merely private, interior way to the individual man, but it is carried by those particularly who "are called": "He called to himself those whom he himself wanted" (Mk. 3, 13). These are the men whom we call "those sent forth," apostles, together with those who continue their office in the history of the world. Here, from another point of view, we have come to the same basic concept as in the second chapter when we spoke of the nature of preaching. Kerygma and apostolic office are the same, and from them is formed the Church. "Herald and apostle,"

136

Paul calls himself (1 Tim. 2, 7; 2 Tim. 1, 11). The body-forming principle of the Church is, therefore, always the word of
proclamation and the ambassador of proclamation—dogma
comprehended in human words, and the men who are the
announcers and protectors of these dogmas, the hierarchy. Both
proceed from the unfathomable freedom of the revealing Trinity;
both become a human reality in Christ Jesus and continue to
live in the Church which is precisely for this reason the
"mystical body." In her the Word of the Logos becomes perceptible for those who are called through the appointed apostles:
"But when God who had set me apart from my birth and had
called me in his mercy, so that I might preach the good news
about him to the heathen . . ." (Gal. 1, 15).

Even within the historical succession of men who carried on
the preaching task there appears a special manifestation in
accordance with the will of the Lord of the Church—a development, as it were, of the visibility to an extreme degree with the
result that we will be able to point out a single person within
the centuries of Church history and say of this person: *This* man
is the guarantee for the purity of all that God has spoken; "You
are Peter, the Rock, and on this rock I will build my Church"
(Mt. 16, 18). On *this* rock, and, therefore, on the line of men
who succeed him as this particular rock until the end of time.
Their perceptible human word binds and looses "here on earth"
what is bound or loosed "in heaven." On this utterly unbearable
and painful becoming visible of the spiritual, invisible, and
heavenly are all spirits distinguished for all times.

Precisely those men of today struggling so very earnestly with
the mystery of the Church—the high-churchmen of England, the
pneumatomachists of the Una Sancta movement in Germany,
the Barthian circle—are scandalized by this visibility of the
papacy (even if for different intellectual presuppositions). Vatican I proclaimed with exalted clarity the theology of the visible
primacy, and to be sure in the same context in which we de-
duced its visibility. Vatican I spoke of the unity and indivisibility
of the episcopal office (therefore of the teaching office) and the
multiplicity of believers (therefore of listeners) and how

unity is preserved by the vital and organic union in the priest-hood so as then to proclaim: "He placed Peter at the head of the other apostles and so established a prepetual principle of this twofold unity and visible foundation" (D. 1821). Thus the fact of the divine word here below is inseparably bound up with the history of a series of individual men who stand in the full light of historical reality, who no longer (somewhat like the history of the episcopacy) are able to withdraw into any circum-scribed responsibility or into the semi-darkness of communal anonymity. These are, rather, those individual men who, to-gether with their personal tendency to error, narrowness, even sinfulness in some cases, are nevertheless truly "representatives" of Christ, and the continuing manifestation of the God-man, even if exclusively in those functions which serve the preserva-tion and continual propagation of the divine word. God has sunk the foundation of the Church so deeply into the visibility of human history that the history of the papacy was and is always also a *proof* of belief because it is in its concreteness never merely a history of the papacy, of the pure and holy and infallible representative of Christ, fertilized by the divine Spirit of infallibility. It is also constantly the history of the popes, singularly involved in the contingencies of political and cultural development and a history of the humanity and sinfulness of these men who are nevertheless designated by God. Through this historical visibility of the papacy our faith must experience the divinity of the Church, and seek it with anxious love. Then loving faith will discover there hidden divinity where dogmatic romanticism wants to see only sanctity and exaltation, only high culture and world-wide influence, and finds the hidden divinity surrendered to the human element. Only in this most bitter visi-bility does the invisible become comprehensible. In the history of the papacy somehow the Word is fulfilled: "The Logos has become flesh, and we have seen his glory." Vatican I spoke in the immediate context of the visible foundation of the Church concerning the future exaltation of the Church which arises from such a foundation: "On the firmness of his faith a Church might arise whose pinnacle was to reach into heaven" (D. 1821). The

Church and the papacy are therefore flesh and glory, or more profoundly flesh because glory and glory because flesh. In our preaching, the visibility of the Church, the history of the papacy, the chapter on the humanity and the weakness of the Church must be related to the mystery of the incarnation of God: "I initiate therefore my path into the history of the Church with the incarnation of the redeemer," says Eusebius in his introduction of his immortal history of the Church.

There is still one more aspect of the profound theology of the visibility of the Church that we must see if we are to integrate our notions of the call, the apostolate, the primacy into which apologetics in its idea of the Church has termed "the perfect society." There were times (and from these times there still live today many whom we have called the pneumatomachists of the Church) when it was forbidden to apply this all too sociological concept to the mystery of the Church. People believed that the mystery of the Church would be vulgarized and made empty through such an apologetic. Today, on the other hand, we see again more clearly that this brilliant teaching about the Church as the perfect society involves something of great significance, if we understand it with its theological overtones in order to keep it from being merely juridical, sociological, or reserved to the apologetic area in which it was constructed. It is precisely here that our theology of the visible must now exert itself in relating the social structure of the Church, and the forms and juridical claims deriving from it to the great mysteries which constitute the nature of the Church. It would be a mistake (and in this lies one of the most hidden dangers to which our love for the Church and our belief in the Church are subject today) to throw off the external forms of the Church's growth, the canons and the rubrics, the Rota and the Index and the thousand other things because they were accretions or at best the cultural sediment of an obsolete age, simply in order to make room for the spiritual house of, say, the Una Sancta. On the other hand, it would be just as much a mistake to equate all these forms and constructs and laws directly with the essence of the Church, and by a type of short-sighted apologetic measure

139

the extent of our love of the Church by the degree to which we assent to all these small and peripheral things. Only dogmatic clarity will give us at this point the correct genuine delicacy with which we will understand on the one hand the ever vital mystery of the Church, while on the other hand we assent just as clearly and lovingly to the "flesh" of the Church today, and consider it as the expression of the innermost nature of the Church as it is being presented *today to me,* and as the unique creation of God (even in all of its limitations and the possibilities for development). "No one ever hates his own person, but he feeds it and takes care of it, just as Christ does with the Church" (Eph. 5, 29). There is a desire in the heart of each of the faithful "to bring the Church to himself in all her beauty" (Eph. 5, 27), a longing for that condition when she will no longer have spot or wrinkle, a holy discontent with the here and now of the Church. Love for the flesh of the Church will never be genuine if these words cannot be forever true of her: "And the Spirit and the bride speak, Come!" (Apoc. 22, 17). But this *Veni* of desire will always become deformed into Adventism if it is not supported by the gracious patience of charity in imitation of Christ who "gave himself for the Church to consecrate her" (Eph. 5, 26).

With the concept "perfect society" are involved the following elements: the number of members, the essential distinction of the members in an organic structure, the unity of the members in a common goal attainable through this distinction, the common effectiveness of the plurality through an ordered principle, and finallly the self-sufficient plenitude of the means which are necessary and must be either within reach or possible in order to attain the final goal. All of this sounds very dry and very cold in our apologetic tracts. But here again it is the aim of our kerygma to sound out its mysterious and joyful significance and share it with men. We must relate what we just said to the incarnate Logos, who as head of all those born of Adam (all men, to whom his general salvific will is extended) joins together his "chosen ones" into the Church by leading them to one, single goal: to be where he

140

is, with the Father, and to "sanctify them in truth." The final goal, therefore, for this "society" is exclusively the sanctification of men in the sense of what we have previously called the "invisible line." A means to this sanctification is the continuation of that proclamation of the Logos's message in history through human bearers, through the instrumentality of all that "he has heard from the Father" (Jn. 15, 15), "for the words you have given me, I have given to them" (Jn. 17, 8). From this instrumentality there results the essential distinctions in membership: the distinction in the structure of the Church between those who teach and those who listen, between the visible body of the Church and its humanly constructed dogma, between the councils and theology, in infallibility and primacy of teaching. Since every word of the Logos proceeds "at the command of Christ" (Rom. 10, 17), this further witnessing of the divine Word is not only a witnessing but a command, a right to power over souls, which proceeds from the "Bishop of Souls" (1 Pet. 2, 25). Thus from this referral of all the visible elements in the Church to the invisibility of the Logos there result the three fundamental building-blocks of the Church as perfect society: the power to sanctify, to teach, and to rule, or to speak in terms of the fundamental charter of the Church's foundation: teach, baptize, and have them all observe all the commands Jesus has given (Mt. 28, 19). With this we have reached the central point of the historical visibility of the Church. *Infallibility, hierarchic structure, power of command* are based on the invisibility of the mystery of the Church, are rooted in the darkly lighted profundities of the procession which the Logos is constantly undertaking from the Father: I have been given all power in heaven and on earth" (Mt. 28, 18). The mission of the apostles of all ages is the becoming visible of him who is the singular "apostle of our faith" (Heb. 3, 1), because he proceeds from the bosom of the Father. The meeting between man and this eternal apostle proceeding from the Father takes place "in the world" through "seeing" and "hearing," through acceptance and obedience in faith: "Whoever listens to you listens to me, and whoever disregards you disregards me, and whoever disregards me dis-

141

regards him who sent me" (Lk. 10, 16). "Who sees me, sees him who sent me" (Jn. 12, 45; 14, 9). "As you have sent me into the world, so I send them into the world" (Jn. 17, 18; 20, 21). "We are God's children. Whoever knows God listens to us; whoever is not a child of God will not listen to us. In this way we can tell what is inspired by truth and what is inspired by error" (1 Jn. 4, 6).

The proximity of God, trust in the Father, and the depths of Christian gnosis are determined simply by the acceptance or rejection of the visible Church, of the word of God which we can hear and grasp. The apostolic succession of the hierarchic Church with all her legal and rubrical forms, her teaching and liturgy, is only the momentary illumination, the incarnation, the taking shape of the Logos who proceeds from the Father and returns to the Father. "Jesus, fully aware that he had come from God and was going back to God, rose from the table, took off his outer clothing, and fastened a towel about his waist" (Jn. 13, 3 ff). This knowledge of the divine mysteries makes it incumbent upon us to speak the depths of God in the human aspects and in the apparently ridiculous insignificance of the visible Church. As Clement of Rome wrote to the Corinthian Christians: "Precisely because we have penetrated deeply into the depths of the divine knowledge we must perform everything in accordance with the ordinance, with the order which the Lord at certain times ordained to be fulfilled" (*1 Cor.* 40, 1). The ancient Church's consciousness of the mystery of the Church has often expressed this synthesis of flesh and spirit and of the Trinity and hierarchy in a profound manner. Ignatius Martyr sees precisely in this synthesis a revelation of his own mystical experience (at a point fundamental for the history of Catholic mysticism): "I cried in her midst, I called with a loud voice, with the voice of God, Stand by your bishop! The Spirit has revealed it to me, in which he therefore spoke; without your bishop do nothing, preserve your flesh as God's temple, flee dissension, become imitators of Jesus Christ as he is his Father's imitator!" (*Philad.* 7, 1–2). "For all who belong to God and Jesus Christ, stand on the side of the bishop" (*Philad.* 3, 2). "All of you ought

142

to obey the bishop as Jesus his Father . . . Wherever the bishop is shown to be, there also is the nation, just as where Jesus Christ is, there too is the Catholic Church" (*Smyr.* 8, 1–2). "Adhere to the bishop so that God will stand by you. I offer my life for those who are supporters of their bishop!" (*Polyc.* 6, 1). Clement, the martyr pope, comprehended this theology of the visible in these words: "Christ therefore is sent from God, and the apostle from Christ. Both occur perfectly in accordance with God's will. While the apostles preach in the country and in the cities, they offer up the first fruits of their preaching to the bishops and deacons of prospective believers" (*1 Cor.* 42, 2–3).

Much is still left to be said in this sketchy attempt to relate the visibility of the Church with all her pressing, burning problems, to the mystery of her invisible nature. It might have sufficed to indicate that here a theological and kerygmatic advance is possible and necessary, beyond an all too vulgar spiritualization of the ideal of the Church, and beyond a faint-hearted complaining about human deficiencies in the Church. The holy Father Lippert has attempted this task graciously and intelligently in the chapters of his book on the Church which he titled "The Church of Law and Officialdom" and "Ecclesiastical Obedience." He concludes the one chapter with the words: "It was a daring decision for Jesus to lay his divine and stainless gifts into the hands of earthly and earth-bound men. This boldness could only be effected by one who possessed a completely reflective, even divine understanding of men who knew that the name of God the Lord is called upon most chastely and reverently by those who are permitted to receive, welcome, and love a man in God's name."[2] This comprehension of the divinely spiritual and yet human and earthly Church is perfected if grace pours into the hearts of men through the mediatory hands of the priest. We must therefore speak, in a future chapter, about the *priesthood* as the visible becoming of Christ.

Yet those basic principles might be developed here which result from what we have hitherto said concerning the shaping of the Church's life. Ignatius called it thinking with the Church.

[2] *Die Kirche Christi,* Freiburg, 1931, p. 163.

143

It will be the newly awakened love of our time. Because it is above the shaping of our kerygma in terms of dogma which concerns us here, the question must then be answered: What follows for our ecclesiastical thought from our reflection on the proposed theology of the visibility of the Church?

II. THE VISIBILITY OF THE CHURCH
AS THE FORM OF OUR LOVE FOR THE CHURCH

We love the Church because otherwise we cannot love Christ. We love her because we know her in faith. Only under her guidance, only because we comprehend her in her visible elements, are we able to penetrate into the depths of the mysteries of God. Cyprian has already expressed this truth with these famous words: "Whoever can no longer have God for his Father cannot have the Church for a mother."[3] This ardent lover of the Church sees the mystery of the earthly visibleness of the Church as one with the mystery of the Trinity: "The Lord said, I and the Father are one. And again this is written concerning the Father, the Son, and the Holy Spirit: and these Three are One. And does anyone believe that this unity originating from the divine stability and closely tied in with the heavenly mysteries can be torn asunder in the Church and be disbanded by the clash of opinions in conflict with one another? Whoever does not adhere firmly to this unity, does not hold firmly to the law of God, to belief in the Father and Son and to life and salvation!"[4] All of the unfathomable mysteries of the invisible, the Trinity, salvation, life can only be comprehended in unity with this visible Church, with the Church of the bishop of Carthage and with the Church of Cornelius in Rome.

This "thinking with the Church" was at all times the characteristic of all the great men in the history of the Church. It is a lofty and proud line of ancestors which was formed by these men with their great love of the Church, and it would be an exalted,

[3] *De Catholicae Ecclesiae Unitate*, 6.
[4] *Ibid.*

enticing task to sketch the history of this thinking with the Church, starting with Ignatius and Irenaeus, continuing through Cyprian and Athanasius, to Augustine and Bernard, up to the other Ignatius who in his writings on thinking with the Church has characterized with mystical precision and holy reverence this interior attitude of mind so difficult to define and yet so unambiguous.

If we are to attempt to deduce the nature of this attitude of mind from this glance at the spiritual history of thinking with the Church, then we must first become quite certain as to what thinking with the Church is not. It evidently consists not merely in the recognition through faith of the Church as the objectively singular means of salvation determined upon by God. Neither does it consist in that excess of ecclesiastical enthusiasm which bids us only to sing her praises.

This attitude which we call thinking with the Church, which is such a pressing, kerygmatic *desideratum* for us, must gradually take shape in us, for we can never dictate and prescribe attitudes but only acquire them. From an historical point of view, we can detect such a spiritual attitude found in the great men of the Church. The martyr Ignatius, who heard the eternal waters murmuring within him, cried out in just this spirit of mystical ardor: "Adhere to your bishop!" Augustine, whose vision penetrated to the depths of mystery and looked forward longingly to the sweet and distant land of the City of God, still cared for his small bishopric in Hippo Regius to his very last breath. Ignatius of Loyola, whose eyes were inflamed by mystical tears and whose soul grasped the mysteries of the triune God in unutterable splendor, organized and worked, wrote letters and directed his attention to this world, threw himself at the feet of the Pope and wandered well clothed through the streets of Rome. These great men could be so complicated because they had become of single purpose in God! For us lesser descendants either the one or the other is ready to slip through our hands. Thinking with the Church in its fullness, however, is the noblest and most spiritually refined perfection of the basic and exalted secret of

145

our Christian vocation: the incarnation. It is really a hypostatic mystery. It is in the realm of the ecclesiastical, what Ambrose says in the hymn: "Let us joyfully drink in the sober headiness of the Spirit, temperate intoxication," the everlasting attempt to link up the headiness of mystery which is present in Christ and in the Church with the sobriety of human limitation, a fact which we experience daily with mute patience, with consternation, and perhaps often with holy anger towards the Church. Pope Leo XIII articulated the essence of ecclesiastical thinking in his encyclical *Satis Cognitum* with these words: "It would therefore be a great and dangerous error if we looked upon the Church either as something completely invisible or if we considered her to be a human institution which consisted of certain life forms and external usages but without the constant pouring in of divine graces and gifts and without the daily proofs of an existence created by God." Thinking with the Church fully affirms the now, the flesh, the visibility of the Church without ever losing the glance of longing "towards the final day" (which has already dawned), as it were the horizontal line of a total view of the Church. It is intercepted by the vertical line, that is, by that attitude which embraces the earthly aspect of the Church's surface and yet is constantly rooted in the depths of mystery which gives meaning and justification to all visible manifestations. Ignatius Loyola has given ultimate expression to this attitude in his rules for thinking with the Church which might be of service to us here in giving more exact shape to our purposes.

First of all, the Church is for him "the bride of Christ, our holy Mother" (*Ex.* 353). At the beginning of all ecclesiastical thought there is reverence in the presence of the great mystery, the fiducial conviction that the breaking of the invisible divine life into the soul takes place only in the community of the Church, that the "spiritual life" is not a purely personal opportunity arising between God and oneself, but "that in Christ our Lord, the bridegroom, and the Church his bride, dwells the same Spirit which guides and directs us in the salvation of our souls" (*Ex.* 365), that sanctified man, the redeemed,

146

can only praise and love God the Father in Christ through the Spirit within the holy community, the Church. Once again we find here what we said in the sixth chapter on the mystery of the Church. But (and this gives thinking with the Church its determined form) this "our holy mother is the *hierarchical* Church" (*Ex.* 353). From this profound dogma of the positions on the Church and her spirit Ignatius immediately concludes to obedience towards the decisions of this Church: "if the hierarchic Church so decides" (*Ex.* 365). Thinking with the Church is never just a wistful waiting for the coming time when only the spirit will remain, but rather the "true attitude of mind we ought to have in the Church militant" (*Ex.* 352). Thinking with the Church is, on the other hand, never the naïve, polemical attitude which makes out of the organization and the Church's struggle almost a "worldly thing." It is never the vital and coarsely vigorous attempt at a union, or the writing mania of some men in the Church who can only picture the Church ultimately as a highly structural organization in which everything "tallies" and is attainable through accurate statistics. Thinking with the Church is obedience out of a sense of mystery. It is enthusiastic, patient, mature, calm, and yet an ardently durable love for the visible. "We ought to praise the singing of hymns, psalmody, the beautiful ordering of the divine worship. We ought to praise the religious life and the vows of religion. We should treasure relics, pilgrimages, indulgences, the lighting of candles in churches, the building and adornment of churches, the pictures and words of penance, fasts and vigils" (*Ex.* 355–356). The visible element of the Church is described here with an astonishing accuracy (even though the selection be conditioned by the times) and taken up within mystery. Church is ever spirit and flesh, love and law, mystery and tangibility. The answer of our fidelity to the Church relative to this incarnational structure of the Church is always both the coolness of reason and the warmth of emotion, obedience and boundless love, reserve and enthusiasm. It is enthusiasm for the Church which takes its source from a dogmatic acceptance of the total nature of the Church,

147

which penetrates all thought and action, and his clarity of faith, joyousness of heart, and Catholic outlook.

But let us attempt now to make comprehensible the nature of this attitude of mind, so difficult to describe, by turning our attention to just how it operates. Ignatius in his great wisdom has given us indications of it. A genuine attitude of mind in this regard is expressed as follows: "We ought to praise *all* the commands of the Church and be always ready to find reasons to defend them and by no means in order to criticize them" (*Ex.* 361). Here there is no question of a polemical enthusiasm which is trumpeting to all its "yes" and "amen," but rather of that love which is anxious because it sees all too clearly, which in its anxiety or dejection still speaks its decisive, yet forceful "yes." For the commandments of the Church possess a sacred consecration of supernatural determination. How can this be, if the visibility of the Church unites itself to the painful nearness of the purely human? "We should be readier to approve and praise the order, recommendations, and ways of acting of our superiors than to find fault with them, even though some of the orders, etc., were or are not praiseworthy" (*Ex.* 362). By no means does Ignatius demand, as some have maintained, that we should praise unconditionally all the customs and edicts of ecclesiastical superiors as good or excellent. On the contrary, his mode of thought presupposes simple, genuine, and sound criticism, and genuine thinking with the Church must not shy away from historical investigation or from firm diagnosis of present human weaknesses in the Church. But from this attitude which alone can produce love, there results here an important conclusion: the correct point of approach to attempts at reform in the Church. Genuine charity towards the Church can never prescind from the here and now for the sake of an exaggerated optimism. It will always "foster the flesh of the Church." It will seek out the weaknesses and sicknesses, the spots and wrinkles of this body, with a holy, timid anxiety of love, and will care for it through a sincere sense of responsibility. It will consequently never cause scandal, a noisy revolt, or a malicious

148

accusation. It will not even offer an opportunity for the crowd because of its own serious anxiety, as Ignatius has so delicately expressed it in the same rule (*Ex.* 362): "yet to speak against them, either when preaching in public or in speaking before the people, would be rather the cause of murmuring and scandal than of profit." All the more respectfully ought we to speak of these things "with just those persons who can apply a remedy." It will finally summon up that divine patience of love, the patience of history which continues along its path in slow measure, apparently undisturbed by the nervous haste with which we want to push along its course (in reality, only those men see it whose eyes have grown in penetration through love for the Church); history is quickened only by men of great love. For the elect have the power "to cut those days short" (Mt. 24, 22; Mk. 13, 20). This attitude must be a burning opportunity for our proclamation of the Church in our days which demand an urgent call of the laity to co-responsibility for the fate of the Church.

Still another manifestation of this theology of the visibility of the Church might be defined here: the basic Catholic "and" in opposition to all cheap heroism of the "either-or" type. Ignatius comprehends this truth for his own time (*Ex.* 363–370) in these contrasted pairs: not only the theology of the Church Fathers but also the assent of Scholastic teaching and the "decrees of our holy mother Church." How fitting this is for the delicate streams of thought in our own time! Further, not only faith but also love; not only grace but also good works. Expressed in contemporary terms, this formulation could mean not only to speak of perfect or "classic" Christendom but also that the less developed, the popular, even the misshapen forms have a validity without giving up the sense of the ideal in tired resignation. Still further, now for the last time appears the mysterious basic law of which we have so often spoken, and which from the time of the incarnation has manifested itself in the constant value and perfection of assent to the invisible and the spiritual through assent to the visible: that the impetus of heroics, the ardor of mysticism, the rays of

149

holiness in the Church are only divine if everything flows from an ultimately kind, patient love for the body of the Church. This has been true from the very inception of the Church. We find witness to this in the Scriptures: "I will pour out my spirit over all mankind" (Acts 2, 17). The spiritualization of humanity can only be completed in the humanization of the Church up to that very day when there will only be spirit. For the Lord, the incarnate one, is spirit (2 Cor. 3, 17). According to his body, and therefore according to the body and the visibility of the Church, his visibility is all judged spirit. "For not everyone who speaks in the spirit is a prophet, but only if he has the way of life of the Lord," *The Didache* (11, 8) says in anticipation of the spiritual experience of 2000 years of Church history. And Cyprian used strong words in this regard: "He cannot be proven to be a martyr who has not held fast to brotherly love . . . Yes, even the gift of prophecy, exorcising evil spirits, doing great wonders on the earth, are certainly sublime and worthy of admiration. And yet one does not attain heaven if he does not keep his path along the straight and correct path, . . . if he sunders the Church, destroys faith, demolishes love, and desecrates the holy mystery of the Church."[5]

[5] *Ibid.,* 14, 15.

CHAPTER NINE

THE THEOLOGY
OF THE VISIBLE SACRAMENTS

In the previous chapters we have considered the Church as the mystery which, since the creation of the world, lay concealed in the depths of God, but which is now made manifest. It is revealed in the physical reality of the Logos and in his life which is continued in the history of mankind. This hidden mystery now becomes "clearly shown" (Col. 1, 26), becomes "luminous" (Eph. 3, 9), and "bubbles up" (Mt. 13, 35) from the depths of the paternal heart. It allows the good Word to spring forth (Ps. 44, 2). The Church is the accumulation of God's mysteries, the great sacrament and visible sign that remains hidden in itself, yet represents the invisible bestowal of grace. It is that sacrament of piety about which Paul speaks in the hymn which contains the entire complexity of that theology which here concerns us: the unity of the flesh and spirit, the emanation from God and the turning back of the mystery made manifest to God:

> *Which was manifested in the flesh*
> *was justified in the Spirit,*
> *appeared to angels,*
> *was preached to the Gentiles,*
> *believed in the world,*
> *taken up in glory* (1 Tim. 3, 16).

This epiphany of the concealed, the incarnation of the invisible, happens in the "now" of the Church, and is found in the men who are "sent." It likewise occurs in the "mystery

151

of Christ which in other ages was not known to the sons of men. It has now been revealed to his holy apostles and prophets in the Spirit" (Eph. 3, 5). The visibility of the Church extends to the visibility of men, that is, to priests who by their words and deeds bear a continual witness to grace and, further, dispense it. Our "visible line" must now extend to the theology of the visible priesthood of Christ, and from there to the visibility of each sign and rite. It further reaches to the visibility of the sacraments by which his priesthood indicates and, in this "indicating," effects the coming of invisible grace. The Trinitarian God has acquiesced so unbelievably in favor of humanity that he not merely places his life in the hands of men, but goes so far as to make it dependent on things, on signs, on rites and whispered words, on water, bread, wine, oil, and chrism.

In the course of this chapter we will first of all treat the important questions relating to the teaching on the "sacraments in general." This makes for a richer dogmatic preaching. Later we will speak about the visible priesthood in the Church and show how this visible participation in the grace-granting dignity of the God-man is a sign among human signs and a witness in living men of the transmission of the invisible life of grace—and is, therefore, a sacrament.

The *Roman Catechism* regards these questions as exceedingly important. They should be "carefully explained by the shepherds of the people" (II, 1, 14). Nor has this directive lost any of its urgency even today. The accurate preaching of this dogma and the care for the visible sign of the sacraments give us a dogmatically balanced middle between the extremes which either contain or produce so many of the problems which arise in the care of souls. On the one hand, one speaks so much today about the inner spiritualization [*Pneumatizierung*] concept of sacrament. People want to be freed from the annoying process of making concrete the devotional element of grace and the sacraments. They prefer to soar into the spiritual heights of a pre-Scholastic or pre-mystic type of thought about sacrament. They do not take notice of the fact

152

that, in the main, they are only reiterating once more what Lutheran theology taught in its teachings on justification and in its concept of the invisible Church. The result is that they avoid the fact that this theology of Luther was never carried to its logical conclusion. On the other hand, there is the even more urgent problem of pastoral theology which stands confronted by the danger of a popularized and all too cheap concretizing of the notions of grace and sacrament. This problem is a source of constant concern for the shepherd as he attempts to bring out the awareness of the inner relationship between the sacramental sign and Christ's dispensing of grace. This is better brought out in the fundamental concept that the indelible unity of the invisible and visible operates in the realm of the sacramental.

In its canons on "the sacraments in general," Trent sketched quite accurately the teachings of the Reformers, teachings which had seemed so spiritual to many. We can best describe this teaching as the "detached visibility" of the sacraments. The process of justification is only realized in the purely spiritualized [*pneumatischen*] field of trusting faith. In this doctrine sacraments are merely external signs which are detached from the spiritual sphere. They are symbols of bare faith, external occasions for the awakening of justifying faith, ceremonies (from which one strangely is not freed in the historical adherence, just as he has not been freed from the structure of the Church herself). They are the characteristics which differentiate the faithful (D. 845 ff.). For Luther the only full-valued "sacrament," the only visible sign of grace being given, is in the last analysis the preached word of God. Consequently, sacraments are, as it were, the sensible word. The preaching and acceptance of the word is considered a sort of sacrament.

Visibility and invisibility are entirely separated. Christ can only be embraced in the word and this only through faith. The encounter of God and man is realized somewhere other than in the visible.

In the same canons previously mentioned Trent gave the opposing Catholic position. It can best be called "a visibility

153

which is bound to mystery." This results in the historically visible link with the invisible. Trent next emphasized the inseparable bond of the sacraments with the notions of grace and justification. The sacraments are those signs "through which all true justification either begins, or having been begun, increases, or having been lost, is regained" (843a). They are signs which signify and contain invisible graces: "If anyone says that the sacraments of the new law do not contain the grace which they signify . . . let him be anathema" (849). This "containing of grace" which is so aggravating to the Pneumatomachists of all times is, meanwhile, understood in its inseparable and never-severed relationship to God who, though unseen, is continually ready to dispense his graces. It is the mystically visible presence of the unity between sacrament and grace. As a result, the council is able rigorously to guard the outward form of this sacramental unity with God, who perpetually dispenses graces (850), because this encounter between man and God's graces does not occur in the purely spiritual sphere of mere faith alone. Consequently, the institution of the visible signs does not give meaning to the somewhat neutral, bare ceremonies; rather, the meaning comes from the freely chosen *placuit* of Christ who has ordered the sacraments, and who lives on in the Church.

Our pastoral preoccupation with the sacraments begins right here. We must impress the faithful with the sort of hypostatic union which exists between the visible sign and the invisible grace. At the same time, we must protect them from an over-spiritualization or despiritualization. That is only possible "in the body of Christ which is the Church." The *Roman Catechism* brings out this idea in one of its most beautiful chapters, the one concerning the sacraments (I, 1, 14). Treated are the internal meaning of the institution of the sacrament, and the wonderful unity between pneuma and flesh, which since the incarnation has been necessary for each encounter between God and man. "In order that we might grasp more easily that which is effected through the mysterious power of God, the most lofty creator of all things has endowed it with higher

154

wisdom. In his benevolent indulgence he makes us familiar with the hidden powers of God through meaningful signs . . . Chrysostom had already expressed it when he traced the visibility of the sacraments back to the mystical body nature of man . . . We are not, he says, made to participate in heavenly blessings by the unadorned, divine pure spirit, but rather by the fulfillment of the visible. We can only rise to the love of the invisible through the visibility of the divine: in word, in miracle, in sacred signs. Even more so is this true in the fulfillment of each sign, which Christ did not institute merely once in history, but which is constantly recalled by his perduring presence in the Church."

This profound chapter of the *Roman Catechism* ends, finally, with a thought which Trent definitely rejects in its condemnation of heretics (D. 849), but which even today invades the truly dogmatic realms. This section rings as a beautiful hymn to the visibility of the Church. The sacraments are signs and symbols of ecclesiastical unity, and the difference between believers and non-believers is a sign, so to speak, of the crisis of the visibility of the Church, a sign of the humble, tangible, and comprehensible spiritual Church, which is widely separated from the spiritual pride of the vociferous yet abject spiritists. "The sacraments check the pride of the human spirit and make us humble, as we are compelled to be subject to the sensible things in order to obey God whom we first of all rejected in order to serve the things of the world." Here that which we can call the asceticism and mysticism of the sacraments becomes somewhat more comprehensible. Sacramental asceticism is the means whereby we, in our own preaching, teach the awareness of the humility of the visible as a continuation of the *corpus humilitatis*. Here on earth we are making a pilgrimage with Christ and the Church. Sacramental asceticism teaches the humble acceptance of grace from the hands of men as well as the unpretentiousness of the outward sign. We acquaint the faithful (but first of all ourselves) with the mystical attributes of the sacraments, with the precious and mysterious depths of the truly godlike work of art of "the

155

greatest artificer of all things," and the power which is behind these symbols. We ought to delineate the meaning of the spirit, the poetry contained in the profound, concrete, visible expression of the invisible in the sacraments. Then we ought to learn to elaborate on the fundamental phenomena of all that is artistic, on the incarnation of the Spirit, where "poetry and prayer" (to speak with Bremond) are linked. Here the fundamental rule which we previously mentioned becomes clearer, clearer perhaps than ever before: whenever man believes that he can do away with the corporeal for the sake of a radically new grasp of the spiritual, he always loses his grasp of the Spirit, of Christ, of the Church, and so too of the sacraments, and ends up clutching ever more vainly at his own fruitless potencies.

I. THE ESSENCE OF THE SACRAMENTS

Of all the dogmatic truths and doctrines concerned with the sacraments we intend to handle only those which are relevant to the construction of our theology of preaching. From the outset it is important to impart to the faithful a concept of the sacraments which is not merely dogmatically correct, but one which is meaningful. We ought to explain what we already know from the history of theology, namely, that the doctrine on "sacraments in general" is the fruit of early Scholastic speculation. Here once again it becomes apparent that speculative theology is really a genuine development of previously revealed truths. It is not a fruitless process of word-splitting but a method we can use to develop a richer and livelier kerygma, and so deepen our understanding of the individual sacraments.

We begin with the definition given by the *Roman Catechism: "Res sensibus subjecta quae ex Dei institutione sanctitatis et iustitiae tum significandae tum efficiendae vim habet."* This definition contains all the well-known truths about the sacraments which we first learned in catechism classes. In the

156

section where the Eucharist is taught this definition is para-
phrased: "the symbol of a sacred thing and the visible form
of invisible grace" (D. 876). It seems ultimately from Augustine and fits very well into the theological formulas which we
attributed to dogma from the outset. A sacrament is the most
visible expression of the invisible. It is the tender surface
of "the body of humility" in which the invisible has been
cloaked. We must emphasize in our preaching of the doctrine
that the sacrament is a "visible sign." We must point it out
as it exists in the God-man relationship, in the revelation of
the incarnation and crucifixion of God, and in the revelation
of the mystery of the visible Church. We must show its validity
in the time of our pilgrimage when we know things only as
"in a dim reflection, as though through a mirror," and do so
till that great day when there remains only "pneuma," when
that which existed and was given under the veil of the visible
sign will reveal itself in the "invisible graces," "justification
and sanctification." The sacraments are, as Tertullian so well
said, "the garment of faith," the veiled mystery of Christ,
comparable to the "loud calling mysteries which are fulfilled
in the silence of God," as Ignatius the Martyr tells us (*Eph.*
19, 1). They are signs of the veiled mystery of Christ in their
mysterious commingling of flesh and spirit, which has meaning only in relation to the incarnation of the Logos. It is this
incarnation which is the source of this unique and powerful
incarnation towards a new formation of life. This sign will
be effected till that very last sacrament is dispensed on the
very last day: "And the old kingdom was destroyed, because
God revealed himself in human form to the new creation of
eternal life. What had been prepared by God began there and
was set in motion because the immolation of death was
undertaken" (*Eph.* 19, 1).

Still more: not only is deeper insight into the link between
the sacraments and the fundamental mysteries of salvation
history significant for preaching on the sacraments, but this
insight also deepens our understanding of the definition. The
sacraments effect the invisible grace through that which they

"signify" at the same time, namely, the Logos. He institutes the "mystical sign" (*Cat. Rom.* II, 1, 12) and is not, so to speak, merely a representative of the absolute divine law who elevates just any sort of sign to the dignity of a power that effects grace. He is the "great artificer" who artistically indicates in sign that which in the divine plan he wants to effect through the sign. Cleansing, refreshing, strengthening ointment, the clasping of hands that are pledged to nourish, give life, and forgive—all of these are signs which indicate the inner meaning of the invisible and lead one first to suspect and then to come to understand what is taking place in the veiled kingdom of grace. This efficacious sign arrives at the primary sacramental event as was alleged by the founding Saviour of the Church. The Church from her earliest days and foremost representatives held this notion of sacramental meaning in word and accompanying rite. For all time these belong to the fulfillment of the sacraments and give us a visible and clear familiarity with the wonderful beauty of the spiritual and invisible. We refer to this divine art work as the liturgy. In the same context as the doctrine of the efficacy which is signified by the sacraments, the *Roman Catechism* says, "The shepherd is not able to err in the fundamentals through which he proves the power of the Godhead and how many rich yet mysteriously hidden miracles the sacraments of the new law adhere to in order to convince all that man must receive them with the highest filial fear" (II, 1, 13). It gives us a firm foundation for holding the accompanying ceremonies in high esteem, referring directly to the "early days of the Church." According to this chapter, liturgy is not just a superstructure of human origin added to the divine simplicity of the sacraments, but rather it is the focusing upon elaboration of what is effected by God in the sacraments. These rites allow the spirit to soar to the heights of the invisible, and they allow reverential fear to penetrate deep into the hearts of the faithful: "They elevate the mind to the loftiest contemplation of things."

Finally, the structural explanation of the fact that there are seven of these signs which were instituted by Christ can distract us from the essential nature of the sacraments which

158

is so fundamental, namely, as the *Roman Catechism* tells us, that they are the inexhaustible sources of kerygmatic preaching. From the fact that in general the visible symbol is an echo of the invisible, and therefore that the natural life of man is a retracing (and so *e converso* the acquisition of knowledge) of the supernatural life "from things which through similitude are transferred from the natural life to the spiritual" (II, 1, 2)—from this fact we develop the meaningfulness of the number seven. It stems from the personal and social structure of man's life: "The light was born, grew, was nourished, was healed, supplemented his weak power, became shepherded by official power, and gives this complete life freely and continuously." That is the sevenfold essence of life which corresponds to that life *qua anima Deo vivit*. These thoughts are all well known to us and we ought not exaggerate their proper theological validity as proofs. The fact that there are sacraments stands uniquely alone among the completely valid proofs of the Church. But in the encounter with our theology of the visible and invisible it becomes clearer particularly if we fall back on those links of which we previously spoke. So too, we realize that human nature was immediately created to bear the supernatural and so was given this power (and without it nature possesses a positive indigence for the supernatural). So it was that Thomas Aquinas, in the same article where he gathered together the thoughts of the magisterium of the Church concerning the number of the sacraments, says, "For the spiritual life has a certain conformity to the physical life, just as other corporeal things have a certain conformity to the spiritual."[1] In our kerygma we must vitalize this mysterious relationship of the mystical signs to the hidden things of the Spirit. The early Church in the richness of her joyful symbols, the rites of the Eastern and Russian Churches, the best of our liturgical movements—all have the proper atmosphere, or else try to acquire it once again. It is here that we arrive at the dogmatic point which enables us to understand the liturgical movement and its loving concern with history. We can better understand

---

[1] *Summa Theologica*, III, q. 65, a. 1c.

the difference between this interest and the eccentric, merely aesthetic, archaic interest in liturgical form. Here we ought to see the source of true liturgical revival as the effort to gain from the visible, outward sign a glimpse of the beauty, the completeness, the pneumatic spiritualization of the invisible. Here for once we ought to be completely poets (if one may so speak), for one day we will all be eternal poets when the spirit has risen and life has devoured death. Tertullian, in his charming "Song in Praise of Water," compared this unity which exists between mysticism and poetry: "At that time the darkness was formless, without the adornment of the stars. Still, the abyss was sad, the earth was not yet finished, and heaven incomplete. The water brought forth completion: it was a material bright, simple, and purified through itself."[2] In the living water of the clear spring the mystics of all time have perceived a rich symbol of divine life, of the Spirit. Water is, as Tertullian mentions in the same work, "the conveyance worthy of God." The Church baptizes with water because Christ so instituted the sacrament, but he so instituted it because, although he is the Lord and creator of all men, he is at the same time divine poet and artist. In *The Didache* one also finds the following said of the visible form of the Eucharist: "A oneness is made from the bread which was once broken and dispersed on the mountains, but which is now brought together."[3] In this section one also finds the almost timid, extremely simple, and on that account deeply symbolic gift of nature, the pure, holy, and immaculate host. And so on with all the other sacraments.

II. THE EFFECTS OF THE SACRAMENTS

We will now say a word about the teachings that concern themselves with the effect of the sacraments. There are three questions which are to be handled at least indirectly: the effect

[2] *De Baptismo,* 3.
[3] 9, 4.

of the sacraments *ex opere operato*, the effect of the sacrament as a communication of grace, and the teaching on the sacramental character.

In our preaching of the dogma of the sacraments we ought first of all to avoid lecturing on the different theological opinions about how the sacraments effect grace. It is much more important to stress again and again in our kerygma the immediate unity of the sacramental sign with God, who disposes the grace. The sacraments contain a power and effectiveness which penetrate to the very depths of the soul. But it is God's prerogative to get into the heart and soul of man, and thus we must believe with completely unwavering faith that he dispenses the grace internally *(Cat. Rom.* II, 1, 23). How this chaste encounter between God and man is realized in the holy sacrament cannot now be grasped by human reason. It is a part of that great mystery which has its effect in us though it "has not yet been revealed" (1 Jn. 3, 2; Col. 3, 3). The manner in which the sacraments effect grace belongs to that life which is still hidden with Christ in God, and whose mysteries will, "when Christ our life will appear" (Col. 3, 4), be encountered in the fullness of divine ecstasy.

This immediacy (as it may always be explained by speculative theologians) between signs, God, and his grace is more precisely expressed by Trent in its defined doctrine on the power of effecting grace *ex opere operato* (D. 851). This dogma, consequently, expressed the tentative speculation of certain schools and raised it, through the teaching of the infallible Church, to the sphere where our groping staff of kerygmatic endeavor can strike the living water from this rock.

This teaching about the effective power which is hidden in the sacramental sign sheds light on the divine geniality which makes the works of pardon penetrate deeply into the sphere of human vision (for the effective dispensing of grace always requires not merely the outward sign, but also the human intention and, where possible, the customary preparation). On the other hand, it is deeply rooted in the invisible power of effecting grace, and its effect itself is in no way engendered by the preparation of man, but joyfully descends almighty and unbidden from the divine heights, where the desire can correspond to human request. Trent's teaching about *opus operatum* is by its very nature directly opposed to the Protestant teaching of justification through faith alone. The time and extent of pardon is not found in the narrow boundaries and indigent power of individual faith (were it great enough to move mountains), nor in the realm of personal pious consciousness. Rather, it is found beyond knowledge, where God alone works, where one is even greater and enlightened by God, a fact of which he is now aware. It is likewise found there in that precipitous depth where the riches of God slowly and with infinite patience settle down to each sacrament in order to first come into the light when the sea of time rolls back and the depths of God yawn open. What humility, and at the same time what raptures must fill us when we consider that God in his sacramental signs is ever so "greater than our hearts" (1 Jn. 3, 2), that despite our earnestness and preparations, we must repeat over and over again—and we ought to—"when you have done everything that was commanded you, say, 'we are unprofitable servants'" (Lk. 17, 10). The teaching on *opus operatum* is nothing more than the mystery of revelation continued into the sacramental. The God who revealed himself and surrendered himself up is no longer the God of our own thoughts, no longer merely the perceived, but the speaking, the greater, the seizer who controls us. Thus we see that it is not through any desire of our own that his power to effect, which involves us immediately with the sacramental sign, and which is not merely measured by the amount of one's faith and love, is called down and admitted. Rather, the effect is wrought through a dominant form in mystical signs which are laden with the divine power of graces which contain what they signify. As Augustine says, baptism is fulfilled *"propria sanctitate atque veritate propter eum, a quo institutus est."*[4] They are effective in themselves

---

[4] *Contra Cresconium*, IV, 16, n. 19.

because they are the sign and word of Christ, because Jesus himself stirs up the love of a man with his mystical presence, and whispers to him his words which bring grace. Relevant to this point, Hugh of St. Victor says that the eyes of the unbelievers see only the visible and do not wish to honor the sacraments of salvation because, while seeing, they do not recognize the invisible appearance, the interior unseen power. They do not know that the faithful do not await salvation because of these things which they ought faithfully to seek out and receive. Thus this wonderful truth about *opus operatum* must be frequently and impressively presented in our own preaching about the essence of the sacrament, about the power which is buried in the sign, and about the power of Christ which becomes active in this sign. Finally, as Möhler wrote in his *Symbolik, ex opere operato* means from the power of him who effects this sign, from the power of Christ.

With that we come to further thoughts which must be brought into our preaching about the sacraments concerning the power of the sacrament to bestow grace. The effect of the sacrament, according to theology, is both justifying grace and special sacramental grace. As to the first: in the Council of Trent it is treated in the discourse on grace (D. 850). Baptism and penance introduce these justifying graces, and the other sacraments increase them, or under certain circumstances give them through their own power. All this is known to us. But our kerygmatic concern is that we bring these doctrines into vital conjunction with all that we previously said of sanctifying grace. For it often happens that the concepts of grace, sonship, and justification become unbelievably empty and lifeless as soon as we speak of them in connection with the effects of the sacraments. For us, grace is the remarkable, mysterious prerequisite for the divine pleasure, a physical accident of the soul, which through the sacraments gives a sort of identification for and legitimate claim on grace. This much we know. Theology had to ponder it wisely and seriously.

What happens in the case of an individual soul who receives the sacrament validly but unworthily (especially in the case of

163

a sacrament which imprints an indelible character)? He receives some impression, which is present before the infusion of grace itself, and through which the sacramental effect can enter the soul just as soon as the impediment of unworthiness is removed. To a certain extent this is an exception which lies outside of the divine plan. It serves to show us how much God wants to withdraw the effect of his mystical sign from the sphere of mere consciousness alone in order to come to his uniquely intended goal. This goal is the influx of grace, as we know if we recall all that we have heard about the miracles of divine love. It is the influx of his Trinitarian life, the dispensing of his spirit, the embracing of his fatherly love, the divine raptures of his very own Trinitarian life in the mirror of creation which he now, even through the visibility of the sacramental sign, insures in the possession of invisible grace. It must not be only a liturgical and historical institution for us, an act by which we sort of return to the institution by Christ, that we dispense and receive the sacrament "in the name of the Father, and of the Son, and of the Holy Spirit." Rather, we must be led, and in turn lead, the faithful into the blessed kingdom where we will see the joyful fulfillment of the unity of the truths of revelation. Never more will they be divided one from the other; rather, they will remain in a "concrete" unity in their full maturity. We now know the sacrament as the filled pool of the established word of Christ the priest which allows the water of the Holy Spirit to run over into souls from the heart of the Father.

Each sacrament further gives a grace proper to the sacrament which the theologians call sacramental grace. We must also preach on that. Here, however, we must protect ourselves from the danger that may also threaten other doctrines, especially the doctrine on grace. We may fall into a certain frame of mind that grace comes in a mechanical way, and the faithful can come to this notion through our presentation when we imply that God must patch up the "mere" sanctifying grace with a special sanctifying grace. Rightly seen, it is much more vital, divine, and human. The sevenfold differences of the sacramental signs show us that God, who dispenses graces, wants to bestow his fatherly love on the children who are loved in Christ in a mysteriously different way. Even though love is inventive and involves more and more novel ways of participation, it is always the same love. Sacramental grace is, therefore, deeply rooted in sanctifying grace. It is one with this grace of the children of God which sets up a claim to the help of the particular actual grace which the Trinity gives in the sacrament. Further, it is an inner self-confidence, a new faculty, or one newly and progressively strengthened as from a font, the immersion of the love of God which we call "participation in his divine nature." Thomas Aquinas calls this participation a "divine help" which is necessary to attain the sensible goal of the individual sacrament—sacramental grace—and gives as an example the peculiar form of grace of baptism: the sins die and we become members of Christ. We can also describe thus the graces given by the other sacraments. In all the sacraments there is the recovered or increased sonship in God but always with a special note: strength and heroism in the protection of this sonship (confirmation), the confidence and vital feeling of being healed in the sonship of God (penance), the bond of love fulfilled in the community of Christ and his members (Eucharist), the ever new enkindling power of the one who is given a mission to testify and give witness to the sonship (holy orders), the sacrificial power in the life long mutual assistance of the community to procreate the child in this natural life (matrimony), and the adjuvant and strengthening of hope in the instant of the definitive choice of filial grace (extreme unction).

When we preach on sacramental graces we must show their intimate link with sanctifying grace. Through our own words we must point up the fact that these wonderful gifts of God are the lovingly solicitous and ever more preserving helps of God for us, and that they are manifested to us in an effusion of life and fire jetting out into our sanctified consciousness from him who is Life (Jn. 5, 26; 14, 25). Paul strikingly described this stimulating and enkindling power of sacramental

165

grace when he spoke of "stirring up again the living fire" (2 Tim. 1, 6). We must make an earnest endeavor to make our teachings about the sacramental character kerygmatically fruitful. This will lead naturally into the topic for our next chapter, the teaching on the priesthood and the individual sacraments.

The teaching of the Council of Trent (D. 852) puts two thoughts before us: the character is an indelible sign, and because of this any sacrament which impresses such a sign cannot be repeated. In both dogmatic facts there lie hidden depths which our preaching ought to probe. But we succeed only if we do not maintain this teaching in rationally categorized disjunctions (as "theses" or "tracts"), through which the doctrine becomes the mysterious presentation of a weak conviction of faith. We also ought to bring out more fully the dogmas about sacramental character, its indelibility, and the resulting unrepeatability of the sacrament. We must show this vital link to the Trinity, which in a new and divine way visibly marks the soul that has been blessed with a glowing finger, and so marks it even if the soul has lost the life of the sonship of God.

First of all, the truths of faith, the character is an "indelible sign." The word "character" is already both serious and awesome. It is the branded sign of God. We must try to let the whole related cultural history of the position of ancient slaves and soldiers come to life. The man with the sign branded on his hand and head is the delivered, the irrevocably committed. He is the man who has made the last, inescapable choice which can only result in victory or death. In the Apocalypse John uses this awesome word when writing about the damned, those fallen to the devil, those men who carry the "character of the beast" (Apoc. 13, 16; 19, 20), but he also speaks of the band of blessed who "did not accept his mark upon their foreheads or upon their hands" (Apoc. 20, 4). The sacramental sign is, therefore, the sign of those men who have fallen to God, that they have "visibly" encountered the merciful God. Character is the sign that clings indelibly to the

166

soul as the proof that those men were once consecrated to God, to the cultic service in the life of the only high priest. The fragrance of this sealing never fades from the innermost depths of such souls. Even the fire of eternal punishment can never burn away, nor can the water of eternal condemnation wash away, this anointing oil of the Holy Spirit, for those men were once immersed in the innermost life of the Trinity and had at one time mixed with God. As the fragrance of incense still lingers in a desecrated church, so there also remains in the eternally damned this "sealing with the Spirit for the day of redemption" (Eph. 4, 30), the sign that one cannot wipe off in eternity, as Cyril of Alexandria so frightfully says. This indestructibility of the character is once again the jealousy of divine love operating in the sacramental realm, because God, who revealed himself and surrendered himself to men, touches mankind with a glowing, piercing finger, and will eternally prohibit this wound to heal, whether it be for the rapturous joy or the burning shame of him whom he had called to his Trinitarian life.

The character is, as St. Augustine says, the "sign of the Lord."[5] the mark that the Lord Jesus Christ impresses, but which remains as indelible as the historical fact of his life and salvific death. Dogma leads us from this quality of indelibility right to the question of the essence of this sign. From this essence arises the further dogmatic truth that the sign-impressing sacraments are not repeatable.

It is of greater significance for the vital kerygmatic development of this truth that we bring the essence of the character into immediate connection with the fundamental Christian dogma of the most blessed Trinity. For this sign is certainly, as we said, the brand of souls who through Christ have broken through to the "inaccessible light" (1 Tim. 6, 16) of God. Now the Logos is in God the "character of the divine essence" (Heb. 1, 3), the essentially similar image of the eternal Father, and in his human nature he is the mediating high priest "who

---

[5] *Epistula 98.*

167

sits at the right hand of the majesty on high" (*ibid.*). Christ's participation in the Trinitarian life, which is granted to his brothers, becomes a participation in this intercessory priesthood of the human nature of the Lord hypostatically united with the Logos. Man, who has been granted grace, is already led into this mediation of the God-man through the fact that he has validly received one of the three divine signs of sonship. He encounters a new relationship to the eternal Father through the pleading elevation of the divine hands of men who perpetually enter the sanctuary for us (Rom. 8, 34; Heb. 7, 25). These hands, though, are pierced and identified through "the mark of the nails" (Jn. 20, 25). Thus it is men who were once upon a time included in this divine priestly prayer of the Logos to the Father in the pierced love of the Spirit (Heb. 9, 11). They were marked, and this mark can never be removed. For Christ "had offered himself once and for all" (Heb. 2, 27), and "once and for all entered into redemption" (Heb. 9, 12).

St. Thomas profoundly explained this relation of the sacramental character to the most holy Trinity and to the priesthood of Christ: "The character is the distinguishing characteristic that is impressed from the 'eternal character' of the spiritual soul. As the picture of God becomes impressed it conforms to the 'prepared Trinity' (the soul) and to 'the created and newly creating Trinity' (of God)."[6] Certainly this is not brought about in the same way as the sonship of grace, but it is a true calling enabling men to participate in the priestly relationship of the God-man to the Father in the Spirit. St. Thomas states: "The faithful are called to and qualified for that which belongs to divine cult, either to receive or dispense to others, and even that occurs through the sacramental character. Now the cultic benefits of the Christian first flow from Christ, the high priest. Therefore, it is evident that the sacramental character is properly the character of Christ, and the believer is formed in the priesthood of Christ through the sacramental sign."[7]

We must teach the understanding of the divine character in

---

[6] *In IV Sent.*, dist. 4, q. 1, a. 2, ad 2.
[7] *Summa Theologica*, III, q. 63, a. 3.

the depths of its meaning. In a true sense that which was written of Christ is true of every man who has received a character-impressing sacrament: "he immediately entered the ranks of the holy." The same is true even if this man is cast out of heaven forever. He was consecrated once, set on the throne of the Father with Christ, and with the high priest entered into the innermost mystery of the All Holy. He remains for all eternity one who was sealed in the mystery.

From this point we can proceed to show in our vital presentation of the revealed truth of dogma, that only three sacraments —baptism, confirmation, and holy orders—imprint a character. We ought to show that the participation in the God-man mediation of Christ in his threefold dignity as king, teacher, and priest, impresses itself in baptism, confirmation, and holy orders. These sacraments build a lasting, cultic unity in an entirely different way than the other sacraments do. Certainly this is significant. But we will make an even greater advance if we give the same thoughts a somewhat different interpretation. The solution can be found in the mysterious words, "he immediately entered the ranks of the holy." The other four sacraments are of their very essential structure terrestrial. They sanctify as long as time for healing remains (penance and extreme unction), but there comes a time when there remains only life or death. The holy Eucharist, mystical and veiled, considers and indicates that it is the most wonderful sacrament, whose complexities will first be fully revealed in the eternal community of love. Still, it is completely a sacrament of this life. For it is the sacrament of nourishment, of growth, of the continuing holocaust which leads to the resurrection. But at some time there will no longer be the Eucharist, no tabernacle, no offering; the priest and offering will once and for all have entered into the All Holy. Then the body of Christ will have achieved the fulfillment and end of the reign of man. There will be no more eating and increasing, but only God all in all. Finally, there is marriage. There remains the life-generating human love which has been so much elevated to the realm of the mysterious. What Christ once said remains true. In the kingdom of heaven after the resurrection one will neither marry nor be given in marriage (Mt. 22, 36). The sacramentally blessed chain of procreation will at some time be terminated. It will be inserted into the midst of the Godhead where our own flesh sits at the right hand of the Father, the first-born of many brothers.

This is not the case with the three sacraments which impress a character. Admittedly, baptism extinguishes sins, confirmation grants strength in battle, and holy orders is a mission "until the end of the world" (Mt. 28, 20). Ultimately, there will no longer be sins, battle, or a mission. But these sacraments are even now totally directed towards the next life. Their essence is not exhausted with the work of salvation which transpires in this time between Christ's resurrection and the resurrection of the flesh of both sexes, which must come to pass for a proper choice. They are sacraments which (to speak with Paul) show that the "coming aeons" are already here, that the mystical sign through which we already perceived the power of the "coming ages" (Heb. 6, 5) is already in effect. The "heavenly gift," the "good word of God" *(ibid.),* now descends to us through these sacraments, as Paul relates with amazing accuracy in a single sentence in which he states the whole process of salvation. It consists of "repentance from dead works and of faith towards God, with instruction about ablutions, the laying on of hands, the resurrection of the dead, and eternal judgment" (Heb. 6, 1–2). Baptism, signing with the Spirit, participation in the eternally dispensing and mediating priestly power of Christ: these are the signs in which occurs the incursion of the heavenly into this world. They are the signs which lift up the earthly and "seat us together in heaven" (Eph. 2, 6) "that he might show in the ages to come the overflowing riches of his grace." Through them we are already "raised up together" (Eph. 2, 6; Col. 3, 1), "living" (Rom. 6, 8; 2 Tim. 2, 11), and "reigning with him" (2 Tim. 2, 12).

The sacramental character is, therefore, in its indelible un-repeatable quality kerygmatically vibrant and can only be grasped through the singularity of the salvific act of the God-man. Through such a sign the consecrated belongs irrevocably to

170

the "Church of the first-born who are enrolled in the heavens" (Heb. 12, 23), to those who have received "a kingdom that cannot be shaken" (Heb. 12, 28). This also holds true if a man made himself unworthy of the eternal grace-filled participation of this kingdom. Keeping these truths in mind we must try to show the faithful that the extraordinary earnestness of Christianity is contained within them, as is the heroic and discerning severity from which the fonts of good fortune break forth. As we are told at the conclusion of the twelfth chapter of the Epistle to the Hebrews: "Therefore, since we receive a kingdom that cannot be shaken, we have grace, through which we may offer pleasing service to God with fear and reverence. For our God is a consuming fire."

CHAPTER TEN

THE THEOLOGY
OF THE VISIBLE PRIESTHOOD

The doctrines about the rekindling of the living waters (2 Tim. 1, 6) is particularly true of the sacrament of holy orders. The sacramental character, as we saw, is a participation in the priesthood of Christ. The vital flood of grace emanates from the priestly heart of the God-man. We find this doctrine enunciated in the theology of the Lateran decrees on baptism: "Here is the font of life, which flows around the whole world. It finds its source in the heart of Christ." Thomas Aquinas had the same thing in mind when he wrote: "The whole rite of the Christian religion is derived from the priesthood of Christ."[1]

The structure of our kerygmatic theology develops consistently. It brings us to the source of the sacred, visible dispensing of grace, to the priesthood as Christ, the only high priest in the fullest meaning of the word, held the office. He allows men to participate in the visible veil of the sacrament, to serve and pass on the further witnessing of his grace in the priestly offering. If, therefore, we trace the wonderful incarnational line of the visible to the humanity of Christ, and then to the human visibility of the Church and on to her visible and audible rite, this emanation of the sacraments from the humanity of Christ becomes revealed to us. At one and the same time, Christ was both priest and offering. He gave himself up to a terrible death which was seen by all, and in so doing he let loose a torrent of

---

[1] *Summa Theologica*, III, q. 63, a. 3c.

invisible grace of the Spirit for the benefit of mankind. "Christ is the source of all priesthood," repeats Thomas.[2]

At this point we might insert a passage from St. Thomas. In the fifty-sixth chapter of the fourth part of the *Summa Contra Gentiles* Thomas sets forth his theology of the visible sacrament. He derives it from the visible priesthood of the God-man. Sacraments, he shows, are those means to salvation through which we immediately contact the grace-giving sacrificial death of Christ. This contact, however, must appear in visible sign because man can only grasp the spiritual in meaningful signs, and because the whole redemptive arrangement proceeds from the Word made flesh. The mystical signs of the sacraments are not merely instruments dispensing grace. At the same time, through their actual ordering of fallen mankind they are also means of salvation. This humble visibility is an antidote for the pride of the spiritual heretics who "want to detach everything visible from the sacraments of the Church." The visibility of the sacramental dispensing of grace is, therefore, in its very depth nothing else than the mysterious continuation of the holocaust which God took on himself in becoming man and dying on the cross, "because in this way they are visible quasi-instruments of God, incarnate and suffering."

We must preach this kerygma of the priesthood of Christ before we speak of the individual sacraments. The intermediary and high priest, Christ must always stand in the center of the doctrine about the seven sacraments. Only in this way can our preaching on the sacraments preserve its internal unity, its compact vigor. The lofty picture of the God-man who dispenses the Holy Spirit from his pierced heart must now inspire the wonderful beauty of the entire dogmatical schema. As St. Thomas says, "So it is apparent that the sacraments of the Church have a special power from the passion of Christ, whose power is in someway joined to us through the reception of the sacraments in whose sign blood and water flowed from the side of Christ as he hung on the cross."[3]

[2] *Ibid.*, q. 22, a. 4c.
[3] *Ibid.*, q. 62, a. 5c.

174

I. THE PRIESTHOOD OF THE GOD-MAN

Where and in what connection we place the dogma about the high priesthood of Christ is of prime importance for the vital formation of our theological structure. For only if we proclaim Christ as the mediator to the heavenly Father, as the priest of heavenly grace, will we protect the fundamental structure of all of our revelation. The "through Christ our Lord" reveals itself to us as the going and praying to the Father through the offered and self-immolated God-man. The grace which is poured out into our hearts through the Spirit of the Father reveals itself as the sacramental visible grace granted through the sacrificial death of the high priest. Without the urgent instructive truth of faith about the priesthood of Christ, the dogmas about the most Holy Trinity and about sanctifying grace remain lifeless oddities. A lack of understanding of this truth leads to that empty, familiar form of Christian piety that no longer has any proper comprehension of the necessity for priest and sacrifice, of the dispensing of grace and sacramental signs. Christian piety today appears to fall short precisely in those areas where the religious practices of classical antiquity, and even of primitive heathen cults, were so vital and active: in their wonderful reserve before the all-holy God whom one can only approach through an intermediary, in their deep-rooted feeling of unworthiness that is expressed through the adoring-offering which is presented, in their deeply human longing after the visible and richly beautiful symbols expressing the encounter with God. Even the rationalists have not yet vitiated these qualities. All of them are fulfilled in a wonderful manner in divine revelation, which is all the more reason why our preaching must once again make revelation ever more vital. We must preach the majesty of the eternal Father, to whom we can now advance through Christ the man and mediary, the offering of the once-in-a-lifetime and mystically ever repeated self-destruction of this man on the cross, the encounter with the eternal Father, the *"propitio ac*

175

sereno vultu" who looks down upon this offering into the mystical sign of the sacrament whose power stems from the sacrifice on the cross.

The priesthood of Christ is the original fact of sacramental giving. Thomas Aquinas says, "It is the essence of the priest to be the mediator between God and the people through the fact that he dispenses the divine to men."[4] "To deliver the divine to the people." This delivery of the divine flows to men from the priestly ordination of the incarnation. The mysterious anointing with the Spirit, which is participated in by the Logos in taking on human nature in the instant of his hypostatic union, is the priestly anointing with the "oil of joy poured before all" (Ps. 44, 7). "Christ is not anointed by men with human oil or human ointment, but his Father who has destined him to be the Saviour of the world anoints him with the Holy Spirit," says Cyril of Jerusalem.[5] This ordination is an anointing for death. Jesus' incarnation was a predestination to the sacrificial death of his human life, and from this priest-offered holocaust, which commences with the incarnation and is immediately given with it, there flows all spiritual anointing which now falls sacramentally to the lot of mankind. The seven sacraments are, therefore, grounded in the holy ordination of the incarnation—and there again in the eternal procession of the Word from the Father, as it is accounted in the Epistle to the Hebrews (5, 5–6): "Christ did not glorify himself with the high priesthood, but he who spoke to him, You are my son, this day have I begotten you." Trent thoughtfully enunciated this early Christian truth. Scripture teaches that Christ becomes the high priest and preaches of our faith (Heb. 3, 1). But he offered himself for us as a sweet fragrance to God the Father (Eph. 5, 2). "If anyone says that the divine Logos did not become high priest and apostle when he took on flesh and became man like us, . . . let him be anathema!" (D. 122). The incarnation of the Logos, who is ever more born of the Father insofar as it is a birth into death, must always be the point of departure for our preaching on the sacra-

4 *Ibid.*, q. 22, a. 1c.
5 *Catecheses*, III, 2 (*PG* 33, 1089).

ments. Here we experience the incursion of the divine into the human, of the invisible into the visible. Here begins the priestly "delivering the divine to the people." From the time of the incarnation there is "spiritual life" on earth; the retaining wall between God and man is breached. The people of God enter into the innermost heaven: "no one ascends into heaven unless it be he who descended from heaven, the Son of man who is in heaven" (Jn. 3, 13). When this Son of man who is in heaven joins with man in human signs, we speak about a sacrament. It is the sacrament brought about by a sign of the Son of man through the heavenly. The community of "the sons of men who are in heaven" is called the Church, who can from now on raise her hands in unprecedented confidence in God, because "the only-begotten Son who is in the bosom of the Father has made him known" (Jn. 1, 18). The Church prays to the Father "through Jesus Christ the universal priest of the Father."[6]

The one who has become man is the "universal priest of the Father." However, it can perhaps be objected that the use of this construct as the framework of our preaching appears to overstress our dependence on the Greek Fathers—or more precisely, that it stresses the meaning of the incarnation at the expense of proper theological emphasis on the crucifixion and the resurrection. The kerygma of St. Paul, it can be said, is put together quite differently in his shaping emphasis on the cross and the resurrection of the body. But this objection is only apparently correct, and does not do justice to the comprehensive understanding of the incarnation among the Greek Fathers. For "to become man" means the totality of the assumed destiny of man by the Logos. Therefore, it means from the very outset "born to die." The visibility of the life of Jesus also culminates in this conception of death, in the destruction of the visible death of the body in order that the invisible, the spiritual, the divine may descend from heaven into Christ the God-man in his visible presence. Becoming man is already an affirmation of death. "The incarnation is born of the virgin," Irenaeus has

6 *Adversus Marcionem*, IV, 9.

said. When we pray that "the womb of the Virgin was not violated," this prayer expresses all of the primitive power of the complete outline of the early Christians which has relevance to the priestly sacrificial birth unto death. "Because Christ has become flesh and become similar to all man, he has been crucified," says Cyril of Jerusalem.[7] Therefore, this truth maintains its eternal validity. Christ saves us through death, and through the immolation on the cross he has allowed the Holy Spirit to pour down upon us. But as death without birth is unthinkable, so there is no birth without death. It is important for the reorganization of our kerygmatic theology that we bring the death on the cross of Jesus (and therefore the perpetually continuing mystical offering, which includes all the sacraments flowing from it) into its proper relationship with the incarnation, with the "today I have begotten you," the eternal birth from the Father. Thus the danger is surmounted that can arise from the differences between the incarnation and the death of the cross, namely, that the mystery of Christmas become diminished to a loving idyll and the immolation on the cross to a merely juridical atonement for blame, with the result that the sacraments become detached from their contact with the wellspring of the supernatural life, which was given for all times when Godhead and humanity embraced each other in an indestructible unity: in the incarnate God, in the mediator, in men, in Jesus Christ.

As the incarnation is a birth unto death, so is the sacrificial death of the God-man a death into life. "I confess the cross, because I would certainly not have owned up to the cross, but I would have concealed it along with my teacher. But since the resurrection followed the cross, I am in no way ashamed to preach about the cross," say Cyril of Jerusalem.[8] Christ himself speaks without hesitation and with divine matter-of-factness whenever he foretells his passion or resurrection (see Mt. 20, 19; Mk. 10, 34; Lk. 18, 33). The hymn of rejoicing follows the death prayer (Ps. 21, 26 ff.). The song about his glorification

[7] *Catecheses,* XIII, 5 (*PG* 33, 777).
[8] *Ibid.,* 4 (*PG* 33, 776–777).

178

follows the prophecy about the suffering servant (Is. 53, 11 ff.). The Son destroyed in obedience becomes "a source of unending salvation" for all who obey him from the time that God pronounced him as high priest of the priesthood of Melchizedek (Heb. 5, 10; 6, 20; 12, 2; Phil. 2, 7 ff.). From his freely willed immolation, from his obedience and offering, there springs the glorification and streams the power even as man to pour forth the Holy Spirit. This fundamental fact of biblical kerygma takes on a new meaning here in connection with the origin of the seven sacraments from the priestly sacrifice of the God-man. The sacraments are in their humble human visibility not only, as Thomas said, the "instruments of God born and suffering," but also "the instruments of glory": as mystical signs through which unglorified man participates in the glorification of the Lord even though it may not "now yet be revealed" (1 Jn. 3, 2). In baptism man is fed with the nourishment of Christ's glorified love of mankind, and imprinted with the sign of the Lord, the character. "Glorification" is the sacramental participation in the *"Kyrios,"* in the Lordship of the *Kyrios* through the "nothing" of the human visible signs which stem from the Lord's suffering and death, "that the life also of Jesus may be made manifest in our mortal flesh" (2 Cor. 4, 11). The sacraments are participations in the sacrificial death of Christ which he himself called "glorification" and which now produces our coming glory. It is even a mysterious spiritualization and glorification of our dead body.

The sacrificial death of Jesus, from which flows the power of all the sacraments, is and remains the focal point of our kerygmatic schema. But it must always be looked at in conjunction with the mystery of the incarnation and resurrection. The visibility of the life of Jesus and the visibility of the Church culminate in the priestly offering of the God-man who sacrificed himself in the freely willed immolation of this visibility and through it now allows the flood of the invisible life of the Spirit to pour out and be seen in order to remodel men in a glorified way to the returning home to the heart of the invisible Father. He sacrificed himself because "it was the will of the Lord" (Is.

179

53, 10), at that time when the thrilling visible continuation of the divine *placuit* broke forth in the economy of salvation. The visibility of this surrender—which we quite correctly call an offering and from which dogmatic theology proves the true sacrificial character of the death of Jesus—was already distinguished by the prophet. He was "a man smitten and brought low, he was wounded for our sins, it was our guilt which crushed him down" (Is. 53, 4 ff.). His body is ransom money (Mt. 20, 28; Mk. 10, 45), a body given over (Lk. 22, 19; 1 Cor. 11, 24), and its blood flowed out, poured out, was squandered (Mt. 26, 28).

In order to grasp more vividly the strong connection between the sacrifice of the God-man and the emanation of the sacraments from this sacrifice, we must in our preaching carefully inquire into the essence of the sacrifice. Here there is another important application of dogmatic theology. We must make the concept of sacrifice more vivid because the visibility of the sacraments is grounded in the visibility of the sacrifice. If in present-day piety there is such a painfully regrettable lack of meaning and necessity for the visibility of the sacraments— which in themselves are so truly human—this situation certainly arises from the fact that our people lack the believing knowledge about the lofty role which sacrifice holds in the honoring of God. St. Thomas Aquinas wrote, "It is a method proper to man that sensible signs be used to express something, because he attains knowledge through sensible things."[9] Consequently, sacrifice belongs to the religious foundation of man. Here, therefore, is an important task for our kerygmatic theology as we endeavor to formulate the notion of offering. In our thoughts on sacrifice we naturally come to the notion of its invisible inner meaning, to the "more internal spiritual sacrifice" which Thomas speaks of,[10] and through which we acknowledge and praise God as the "creating beginning and blessed end." But the consciousness must become stronger in today's Christians, who must express the mental attitude of worship in something visible and tenable.

[9] *Summa Theologica*, II, q. 85, a. 1c.
[10] *Ibid.*, a. 2c.

We must approach God bearing a gift that is valuable to us. Our kerygma must inform the faithful why we Christians present an interior sacrifice as a holy and heavy burden on our fallen consciousness. We who in trembling reverence and holy anxiety must seek a gift worthy of eternity, are far from God. At the same time, we are the blessed of the Lord who bear the one offering worthy of God, the Immolated, and are made acceptable to God through the sacrifice of the immolation-glorified body of the God-man. Sacrifice is the irrevocable consecration of the humanly visible gift to the eternal God, a consecrated present of the visible gift to God in recognition of his almighty power and excellence. The awareness of the obligation of sacrifice has been dulled because our preaching has long lacked a courageous large-minded emphasis of "God's honor." All sacrifice is "in the glory of the Father," "a thanksgiving for your great glories." But the picture of the "loving God" has become too commonplace for many Christians, and the Christian rite of candid reverence before God has disappeared, so that the faithful have lost that very important knowledge of our human separation from God. Diminished also is that sweet awe of the proximity and trust of God in which we are incorporated through the sacramental contact of God in the power of the sacrifice of Christ. Therefore, in order to make our preaching about the sacraments more fruitful we must not only connect the sacraments with the sacrifice of Christ, but also further the understanding of this sacrifice through a most profound awakening of the understanding of the notion of sacrifice itself. Our kerygma ought once again to explain the incarnational link between visible and invisible, between the interior sacrifice of our reverential unreserved worship of the All Holy and the "visible sacrifice" of Christ. This is what St. Augustine had in mind when in *The City of God* he gave his famous definition of sacrifice: "The visible sacrifice is the sacrament of the invisible sacrifice, that is, it is a sacred sign."[11]

[11] X, 5.

II. THE SACRAMENTAL PRIESTHOOD

We have seen that the priesthood of Christ is "the original source of all Christian cult," and that the sacraments create their power from their vital link with the priestly offering of the God-man. We come now, in the logical progression of our theological schema, to speak about the sacramental priesthood as the first of the sacraments. Certainly we could also begin with baptism as the fundamental sacrament, as the mystical sign in which men receive the gift of participation in the divine nature in Christ. It is the source where, for the individual man, the life of the Holy Spirit begins to spring out of the sacrifice of Christ, visible in a sanctified symbol. That view would be individualistic. We still want to look at the organic structure of the salvation economy, for it exists for the whole mystical body of Christ. Here a frequently overlooked fundamental truth comes to mind, namely, that the divine life in Christ fell to the lot of his brother men instantaneously because Christ, in becoming man, was anointed high priest of all mankind. The first sacrament is, therefore, the priesthood of Christ. It is not as though Christ, the man, had received a sacrament, for in the power of the hypostatic union with the Logos the man Christ is substantially priest. Therefore, he needs nothing of the impressed sign of the priesthood. He is, essentially and above all, a priest, and thus the *Roman Catechism* has accurately grasped the kerygmatic structure of this truth of the faith when it teaches: "If one attentively considers the nature and essence of the other sacraments, it will readily be seen that they all depend on the sacrament of orders to such an extent that without it some of them could not be confected or administered at all. Still others would be deprived of all of their solemn ceremonies, as well as of a certain part of the religious respect and exterior honor accorded to them. Wherefore, in continuing the exposition of the doctrine of the sacraments it will be necessary for pastors to bear in mind that it is their duty to explain with special care the sacrament

182

of orders" (II, 7, 1). The sacramentally visible witness to the invisible life of grace emanates from the visible priesthood of Christ and becomes transmitted to those men who in a visible sacramental way obtain a share in the priesthood of the God-man. This priesthood is petitioned and granted to them. The sacrament of holy orders thus is the visible continuation of the priestly visibility of Christ rooted in the incarnation, and there flows from it, through all the time of human history, the power for the transformed sanctification of the whole race that is chiefly projected into the deepest recesses of the Trinitarian Godhead. "And so it is that all sanctification which comes through his priesthood is perpetual and remains a consecrated thing," says Thomas in connection with the indelible character of the priesthood.[12] "Through the sacrament man is commissioned to dispense the sacraments to other men."[13]

Our first kerygmatic application relating to the sacrament of orders is to explain the essential and unbreakable link of the priesthood with the visible priesthood of the God-man. In this way the priest can better illustrate how, through the mediatorship of the Lord which binds things on earth and in heaven, the sacrament of holy orders is the source of the other sacraments. The inner teleology, the cosmos of the seven sacramental signs, becomes visible for the first time in union with the Logos who has become flesh.

The sacrament of holy orders is the continuation of the priestly visibility of the God-man. Thomas enunciated this truth quite profoundly in the wonderful chapter of the *Summa Contra Gentiles* (IV, 74) which treats of ordination. "Since Christ withdrew his corporeal presence from the Church, it was necessary that he put on other men as his representatives, men who could dispense the sacraments to the faithful." This representative continuation is necessary in the exact sense which he explained shortly before (IV, 56) in his theology of the visibility of the sacraments, which is also derived from the incarnation of the Logos. The graces of God can only be dispensed by living

---

[12] *Summa Theologica*, III, q. 63, a. 5c.
[13] *Ibid.*, a. 6c.

human hands, they can never be dispensed solely on the ground of an historical law of a previous era that exists now merely on paper. What we have said of our theology of the visibility of the Church comes once more to the fore. The Church as the living prolongation of the incarnation can only be formed by a living man. Only men can pass on graces, because the divine grace gushes from the pierced hands of a man and the flood of living water rushes out from the heart of a man on earth, in order to save others. The necessity of the visible priesthood depends on the inner linking of the Logos with the incarnation and, with that, the essence of the visible and audible dispensing mystical sign, the sacraments. Thus there is a need for a continuous chain of men who are signed with the Logos—which leads St. Thomas to conclude, in the same chapter of the *Summa Contra Gentiles,* that the essence of the representative priesthood is as a copy, an instrumental assimilation to the Logos become flesh. "It is necessary that an instrument conform to the essence of him who is handling it: the priest must be of the same form as Christ. But Christ, as the Lord, has wrought our salvation from his own original and complete power and strength because he was God and man. For as man he has directed our salvation, but because he was God he had the salvific power of this suffering. Therefore, the priest of Christ must be a man, and nevertheless one who has a share in the Godhead through the power of his spiritual office." In this wonderful description the whole mystery of the priesthood lies hidden, both in its dogmatic and ascetical aspects. Thus we must preach to the faithful: "It is proper that men be ministers for Christ and participate somehow in his divinity." The priest must be a man, a flesh-and-blood man who is human in the fullest intellectual and emotional senses of the word, because he represents the man who gave the world salvation. The priest must also be a Godlike man, because his humanity ought always be only the historically tenable visibility of the invisible Logos, the transparency of the inaccessible light in which God lives. The priest is, in truth, the "Logos become flesh." His full and real humanity is in no way a retrogression to any sort of richly sweet (and, in the last analysis, bloodlessly rationalistic) humanism, but a new descending from the heights of participation in the Godhead, a descent into the human. The priest ought to be as Moses shining in his descent to the lowlands from the dark heights of Sinai; as Christ, kind and healing, returning from the apparition on Tabor. This is what Ignatius the Martyr meant when he wrote, "Let me receive a pure light, for when I have arrived over there I will be a true man" (*Rom.* 6, 2). "His deification ought never be denied of the human. He must be a man whose soul shines with beauty in order to edify and illuminate the hearts of all who look upon him," as Chrysostom says. A lively testimonial of our kerygma is that we no longer form the preached word solely out of the original sources of revelation, but show that preaching must start personally with the priest who is preaching. For that very reason, Christ has for all times entrusted his word to his priests. The effective power of the word is dependent on the thorough formation of the priest in conformity with the "incarnate" basic structure of the Word become flesh.

It is obviously imperative, therefore, that in our kerygma we provide the faithful with a solid understanding of the essence of the priesthood, one that is not only dogmatically correct but also more "edifying" in the true sense of that New Testament word. The early Christians had a true dogmatic and pious understanding of the priestly mediation of the God-man for the Father, but before long there came that "terrible hour" about which Chrysostom writes in his work on the priesthood when the sacramental priesthood came to achieve an absolutism of its own, and the priest became the earthly co-producer of some angelic worship to the triune God. "The Paraclete himself instituted this office," says Chrysostom, "and fills men, who still live in the flesh, full of power to perform the work of angels."[14] The priestly sacrificial service becomes almost (not, of course, in any dogmatic conception, but in emphasis) the absolute offering. With trembling reverence Chrysostom writes, "The office of priest is one that is so high that no nobler function than theirs

---

14 *De Sacerdotio,* III, 4 (*PG* 48, 642).

can be imagined. Justly, therefore, are they called not only angels, but even gods, because of the fact that they exercise in our midst the power and prerogatives of the immortal God." No doubt, it is generally this kind of conception of the priesthood which most of the faithful have. It is the kind of thinking which a priest encounters in his family, much to his chagrin, at the time of his first Mass. The esteem of the faithful for the priesthood should, of course, always be encouraged—but it should also be enriched by a doctrinal understanding of the place of the priestly work in the plan of salvation. We must emphasize in our preaching, therefore, that there is only one sacrifice, the sacrifice of the God-man on the cross. The priest is the visible representative of the one priest, Christ, whom the Lord God endowed with the highest authority to dispense graces and forgive sins. The Lord left this authority to the Church even though it is a restrained power, one bound to the sacraments. So it is that especially picked servants are set aside to practice this authority, and they are ordained to this duty in a festive ceremony. This consecration we call holy orders. Our kerygma should preserve the balance, the divine-human measure between a piously exaggerated authoritarianism whereby the "people" are kept at an all too great distance from the sanctified realm of the priesthood, and an exaggerated de-emphasis on the differences between priest and laity. Certainly it is more important than ever to instruct the laity of their kingly priesthood. "All righteous men have priestly rank," says Irenaeus.[15] "Christ holds without difference the graces of the priesthood for all who wish them," says Gregory of Nyssa.[16] The *Roman Catechism* states this profound teaching even more accurately: "All of the faithful are said to be priests, once they have been washed in the saving waters of baptism. Especially is this name given to the just who have the Spirit of God, and who, by the help of divine grace, have been made living members of the great high priest, Jesus Christ. Enlightened by faith which is inflamed by charity, they offer up

[15] *Adversus Haereses*, IV, 17.
[16] *De Oratione Dominica*, III (*PG* 44, 1149a).

186

spiritual sacrifices to God on the altar of their hearts. Thus we read in revelation: 'Christ has washed us from our sins in his own blood and has made us a kingdom and priests to God and his Father' (Apoc. 1, 5–6)." The *Roman Catechism* might well have added: in the preaching of these truths the essential difference between the general priesthood and the sacramental priesthood should ever be clearly and emphatically enriched. It is a common notion today that the dogmatic essence of the general priesthood can best be understood if the meaning of the sacrament of orders is minimized. According to this notion, the activity of the ordained priest is limited to the purely sacramental area and shows equality of birth with the lay priesthood with reference to the time of the early Church. At one time each baptized person was himself a missionary, who considered himself a "sent" (read: "ordained") emissary of the gospel, and he acted as one.

This line of reasoning is, however, both dogmatically and historically incorrect. In the first place, the priesthood of the laity can in no way be understood to stand in opposition to the sacramental priesthood. Two things must be stressed: the magnitude of the sacramental priesthood, and the fact that the priesthood of the laity is not "of equal value" with the sacrament of orders. It is an erroneous belief that without the mediator Jesus Christ, and without the mediation through the visible sacramental priesthood, man can still converse directly with God through trusting faith. For only those who are in Christ, the man, rest in the midst of the innermost Godhead. It is also wrong to believe that there can be a fundamental grace-dispensing contact with the divine that is separate from the sacramental priesthood. "Only the priest who consecrates the Eucharist, which is the sacrament of the whole Church, has the act of the whole Church," says St. Thomas. The Christian who remains in grace is a priest in Christ through baptism, but there is a clear distinction between this priesthood and the sacramental priesthood. Our kerygma must lucidly certify the individuality and at the same time the life-generating composite of both of these priesthoods as they exist in the body of Christ. Only thus do we watch over the believing and spirit-filled understanding of the "divine hierarchy" of the Church.

Only after we have recognized the priesthood of the God-man and its visible sacramental continuation in the sacrament of orders—which is deeply rooted in the sacrificial ordination of the incarnation—can we understand and preach the development of the invisible life of grace which pours from the priesthood into the other sacraments. The visible through which we "become carried away" to the "love of the invisible" is the body of Christ, the sacrificial body of his humanity and the mystical body of his Church. The sacrament of orders finds its purpose in the body of Christ, in the reality which is hidden in the most exalted sacrament of the Eucharist through which the mystical body is developed and nourished. "The power of orders is ordained to the dispensation of the sacraments; however, among the sacraments the noblest and most consummative of the other sacraments is the Eucharist. It is fitting that the power of orders can be considered especially according to the relationship of this sacrament, for each sacrament is ruled by its end." Thus says St. Thomas with his incomparable clarity. What binds all the other sacraments together is the link between the visible mystical body of Christ and the eucharistic mystery, which proceeds from the central mystery of the incarnation where all visible and invisible find their goal and origin. The sacraments are the visible signs of a mysterious power. From them the body of Christ constantly replenishes itself, and through them Christ is perpetually born in the hearts of the faithful. "Which we perceive while handling the visible mysteries and are led to the invisible effect," prays the Church. The priestly ordination of the incarnation of which we sing in the hymn "Virginis sacrario intacta prodis victima," the birth unto death and the rebirth arising from the sacrificial death to the glorification of the resurrection of the body, are together the prototype which matures into the power of the offered eucharistic body, into the conclusive glorification. Scheeben has impressed these ideas in words which are ranked among the best ever written on this subject. This blessed kerygmatic writer says, "The ecclesiastical priesthood should regenerate Christ himself in the womb of the Church—in the Eucharist and the hearts of the faithful—through the power of the governing Spirit of Christ that is in the Church. The priest through the power of this same Spirit conceives the Son of God, who has become man, in order to place him in the womb of the Church under the eucharistic form. Through the priesthood Christ is born again, as it were, through a continuation of the wonderful birth from Mary."[17]

[17] *Mysterien des Christentums,* p. 79.

CHAPTER ELEVEN

THE THEOLOGY
OF THE REMAINING SACRAMENTS

The body of Christ and the eternal life emanating from the priesthood of Christ and living on in the Church: these are the two mysteries which we must now speak about in order to complete our kerygmatic construct. "Body of Christ" as the goal of the development of the salvation economy matures into the sacraments, and "eternal life" is the invisible goal of the body of Christ in its sacramental construction. Thus we should treat of the individual sacraments not only in their detailed individuality, since individually they exist in the body of Christ and lead to eternal life; but we must also learn to comprehend the sacraments in their inner relationship, both mystical and sacramentally physical, to the mystical body.

All sacraments have their origin in the priestly sacrifice of the God-man who "suffered the incarnation" and who perpetually renews this sacrifice in the sacrament of the body of Christ, through which the mystical body of the Lord grows and advances to glorification: unto eternal life. Chrysostom has spoken of this origin of the sacramental life, and of the beatitude coming from the priesthood of Christ and the priesthood of the sacramentally ordained representative of Christ: "For if no one can enter the kingdom of heaven unless he is born again of water and the Holy Spirit, and if everyone is excluded from eternal life who does not eat the flesh of the Lord and drink his blood, and if these things are brought to completion through no one else than through those holy hands—I mean the hands of the priest—how can anyone escape the fires of hell without

191

them or attain the crown which was prepared for him? There are, nevertheless, priests who have consigned themselves to the spiritual birth-pains, priests to whom it is granted to generate new life through baptism: through which we put on Christ, become bound together with the Son of God, and become parts of that spiritual head."[1]

Our main stress will be on the progression of the line that binds all of the sacraments together. We will show how the individual sacraments pour from the priestly hands of the God-man as the humble signs "of the God who becomes flesh and takes on a body" in order that the glorified result of the sacrifice of Christ be communicated to the mystical body. We will also explain how here on earth the sacraments are arranged in the august sacrament of the Eucharist, even though in a veiled way, and how the glorified body of the Lord descends into our still unclear visibility.

First of all, we take up the sacrament of matrimony. It is not that we want to reverse the honored ordering of the sacraments as put forth by the Council of Trent. We begin with the "last" sacrament because the unpolished form of our theological construct depends on the emphasis of the kerygmatically fruitful relationships with this sacrament.

The sacrament of matrimony is that "radical mystery" of the salvation economy. In the original plan the supernatural sanctification of humanity destined a sexual relationship from which humanity would unfold and concomitantly would come the sublime work of further generating the supernatural. Immediately, by belonging to the race of Adam, men would become children of God. Generation and delivery were taken from the outset into the depths of the divine mystery. In the new order of salvation, participation in the kingdom of grace is no longer bound immediately to the generation from the race of Adam, but to the "second birth" of water and the Holy Spirit. But natural marriage remains in itself a last wonderful glimpse of a lost beauty. Wherever two persons lawfully bind themselves to

[1] *De Sacerdotio*, III, 5, 6 (*PG* 48, 643).

this community of loving generation of new life, they fulfill the replica of a mystery: that of the incarnation, which leads to birth and life, in the succession of normal generation, through the generative power of Adam. Through the incarnation Christ brought the human race into deep loving union with the Trinitarian God. "This mystery is great and certainly on account of his relation to Christ and the Church," says the apostle (Eph. 5, 32). Natural marriage is already a true likeness, a peaceful aftereffect of the original mystery of the divine plans for salvation. If the mystery of the sexual life in the new order of salvation no longer holds the immediate power to generate the supernatural life, it is nevertheless moved up even higher in the sanctified domain of God because of the fact that marriage has now become a sacrament, a grace-effecting sign, and it reveals its deepest essence in that same image which portrays the unity of Christ and the Church: to be the visible sign of that invisible grace which enables both of these people to form a deeply rooted union with the body of Christ and certainly with that love of which it is written: "Husbands, learn to love your wives as Christ loved the Church and delivered himself up for it so that he might sanctify it" (Eph. 5, 25).

It is the task of our kerygmatic construct to show the close relationship of holy matrimony to the mystery of the sacrificial incarnation and to the coming glory of mankind. In the first place, then, matrimony is a sacrament only for the baptized and insofar as baptism is objectively and logically the first sacrament. But on the other hand, marriage grasps out into the sanctified domain of the kingdom of God. While that new life engendered by marriage certainly stands outside of grace, it prepares as it were the physically visible matter in which the miracle of rebirth and participation in the body of Christ takes place. For through the descendency from each marriage, man becomes the blood-relative of the God-man—and without this lineal blood relationship with the second Adam through the first Adam, the return to grace, which stems from the blood of the God-man that was poured out, would be impossible.

In the womb of the Virgin Mary God mystically married himself with our mortal nature and, with this marriage, fundamentally raised the whole race, which would unfold in sexual reproduction from Adam on, and proceed to the kingdom of grace in order to make this flesh immortal. For this reason, God has elevated the marriage of baptized persons, the germ cell of mortal flesh, to grace-effecting mystery. Augustine expresses this truth eloquently in his *Confessions:* "But he came down to us, who himself is our life, and took our death away and killed it by the overflow of his life, and with the voice of thunder he calls to us that we should turn back into that hidden sanctity from which he stepped forth into the body of the Virgin where he married himself to the human nature, the mortal flesh from which fact it remains no longer mortal."[2] The sacramental marriage is, therefore, the "sanctified seed-bed of the human race," as Tertullian says.[3] It is sanctified through Christ, the Incarnate, who descended to us, who participated at the marriage in Cana, "in order to sanctify the fundament of human generation so far as the flesh comes into consideration, in order lovingly to prepare the loving grace," as Cyril of Alexandria has said.[4] In the face of such mystery, we must newly inflame our preaching with this holy reverence: that men are called to and qualified to generate new life, life that will linger on into eternity, that will be called into the mystery of the Trinitarian God. We must preach that every birth is the beginning of a never-ending eternity of happiness or unhappiness. We must preach that each man is related by blood to the Incarnate according to the flesh, and is called to participation in the body of Christ according to the Spirit. Finally, we must preach that this new life should be constructed in the Church, who took her source in the womb of the Virgin and was born in the pain of salvific suffering, and who now through the power of this sacrificial incarnation wanders into the eternal life of the glorification. "The Son of God goes to the nuptials so that what he established by his power would then be sanctified by the blessing of his presence. He goes to the

2 IV, 12.
3 *Ad Uxorem,* II, 1.
4 *In Joannem,* II, 2, 1–4 (*PG* 73, 224–225).

nuptials of the old dispensation and by his going makes a new spouse of perpetual virginity for himself from the conversion of nations."[5] With these words, Maximus of Turin preached the mystery of marriage in its sacramental difference from natural marriage.

This is the sacramental intent of marriage: the maternal preparation of the members of the body of Christ. The intent stems from the matrimonial mystery of the incarnation. The incarnation turns death into life, death into glorification. "For thus has marriage been elevated to the dignity of a sacrament," according to the Council of Trent, "in order that from it may be generated and educated a people to the service and reverence of the true God and Christ our Saviour" (II, 8, 15). Trent expressly attributes the sacramental grace of matrimony to the sacrificial suffering of the God-man. "Christ himself, who instituted the holy sacraments and brought them to perfection, merited for us by his passion the grace that brings natural love to perfection, and strengthens the indissoluble unity, and sanctifies the spouses" (D. 969).

Because the growth of the body of Christ can have no other object than the glorified reordering of mankind for the days of glory, the sacrament of matrimony is to be preached in its relation to the total glorification of our race. At the end of the act of faith we pray, "I believe in the resurrection of the dead." But the flesh, whose glorified resurrection we long for, is the same flesh which originates through marital union. Two baptized persons unite themselves to generate a new life in marriage. When they dispense this grace-bearing mystical sign to each other with royal and priestly authority, and so sanctify in Christ the origin of generation, they do so only because their own flesh and blood which now lies peacefully in the hidden womb of their sexual power, is the same flesh about which we confess, "I believe in the resurrection of the body." Whenever we begin to speak of the rights and duties of marriage and about the canons on marriage law, we must take notice of this wonderful outpouring of grace,

[5] *Homiliae*, 23 (*PL* 57, 274b-c).

195

the whole eternal formal authority, the eschatology of marriage which God has placed in the hands of men. In a word: the body of Christ, and eternal life, is dependent on this sacrament. Marriage is, therefore, a "great mystery in Christ and the Church."

From the sacramental sanctification of the origin of all birth we can rightfully proceed to speak of the sacrament of "rebirth in the Holy Spirit," about baptism and its fulfillment, confirmation. In this connection it is impossible to do anything more here than merely indicate the main points of a kerygma of baptism. We must content ourselves to lay open the inner structure of both of these sacraments. We must look at their relation to the construction of the visible body of Christ, whose glorification likewise stems from the ordained death of the incarnation and the glorified sacrifice of Christ. So, too, we must investigate their relation to the sacrament of the body of Christ.

The body of Christ and the eternal life are the truths which point the way to the fundamental sacrament. Baptism is first of all the sacrament from which the mystical body is built. In the kerygma of the Church Fathers, no point is more frequently mentioned than this: that baptism is the mystical, sacramental continuation of the incarnation of the Logos from the Blessed Virgin. As Mary produces the physically salvific body of the Logos through the power of the overshadowing Spirit, so the mystical body of Christ now grows through the power of the same Spirit through its birth from the virgin mother the Church. "The earth of human flesh," wrote the saintly Pope Leo the Great, "which had been cursed by the first sin, has brought forth alone in the womb of the Blessed Virgin a sprout which was blessed and was spared from the strain of his race. Each one receives his Spirit-effecting source in the rebirth. For each man who comes to the rebirth, the water of baptism is a replica of the virginal womb; the same Holy Spirit who fertilized the Virgin fertilizes the fonts of baptism . . . The same sort of origin which he took in the womb of the Blessed Virgin he placed in the source of baptism. He gave to the water that which he gave to his mother."[6]

[6] *Sermo,* 24 (*PL* 54, 206a).

196

The incarnation of the Logos was a birth unto death. Thus to our perishable bodies baptism is an image of his sacrificial death, and the baptismal grace is a font of the living water flowing from his pierced heart, a priestly participation in his suffering, a signing with the suffering of the Lord. Cyril of Jerusalem tells his catechumens that "with your death follows your birth. That saving water becomes both a grace and a mother for you."[7] We are all rebaptized in the death of Christ (Rom. 6, 3–4). That humble, plain sign of water which Tertullian so thoroughly defended is a sacred symbol of the immolative death of the high priest Christ. In our baptismal kerygma we must show the faithful the need for suffering. The baptized is the priest: in his mortal flesh he must suffer with the suffering Christ and be fulfilled in the suffering of Christ. This suffering veils the baptismal glorification. Baptism is an ordination to death because the incarnation was a being born unto death. Baptism is a unifying of the heart with Christ the priest: all graces find their sources in his heart. As the baptismal poem of St. Leo says, ". . . finding its primacy in the wound of Christ."

Baptism is a mysterious and hidden glorification. The body of Christ which increases through baptism is still a body of humility, visible in its historical immolation, in the fated suffering of the baptized individual. But the tremendous power of glorification has already invisibly affected us since the day of baptism. In that divinely lofty dialogue on the day of our baptism, the Church told us how the humility and immolation of faith, the joyfulness of eternal life that is still veiled in shadows, should mature: What do you ask of the Church of God? Faith. What does faith hold out to you? Life everlasting.

The mystery of glory is effected with divine secrecy in the humble waters of baptism. "May this cause the presence of his glory," says the prayer for the blessing of the water in the Ambrosian liturgy. That a "heavenly race" be torn out of the water is the prayer of the Roman Church. St. Leo the Great in his song of baptism intones the desire for a "people destined for heaven, springing from the holy seed, bringing the Spirit from

[7] *Catecheses,* II, 4 (*PG* 33, 1080c).

fruitful water." The baptismal enthusiasm of the early Church is grounded in this desire, and must be newly awakened in our baptismal kerygma. The mystery of glory is already there. It is not just coming for the first time, but always coming: "as Christ is risen from the dead by the glory of the Father, so we may also walk in the newness of life" (Rom. 6, 4). Our sermons on baptism ought always to close with the words which Cyril once spoke to his baptized: "God, who has awakened you from death unto life, granted you the power to give grace, to wonder in the newness of life, for it is reverence and glory to him now and forever."[8]

It is known that in the early Church, confirmation was conferred immediately after baptism. Rebirth and its fulfillment were at that time (and are today and always) dogmatically a liturgical unity. The sacred mystery of birth and anointing with the Spirit was recognized. "After the fact it remains for him to become perfect," says Ambrose.[9] With us too, the mark "confirmation" customarily indicates the inner relationship to baptism. The grace of this sacrament is the "strengthening" of the grace of baptism, the unfolding and fulfillment through the anointing with the Spirit. So it is that the Council of Trent joins the three canons on confirmation immediately and without transition to those on baptism. Our kerygma on baptism must conform completely with this innermost relation of confirmation to baptism. This means that here we must clearly enunciate the ultimate goal of this holy sacrament, which is the formation of the visible body of Christ and the glorification of this body in eternal life. This is of great importance today precisely where the questions and problems about a new structure of confirmation and the catechetics related to confirmation are vigorously discussed and where the practice of the Church is more and more frequently returning to early confirmation. One of the many problems that burden the pastor is that he must take pains to prevent confirmation (certainly not in a dogmatic sense, but in order better to form it liturgically) from becoming a ceremony

[8] *Ibid.*, 8 (*PG* 33 1084b-c).
[9] *De Sacramentis*, III, 2, 8, (*PL* 42, 1093).

198

which makes no impression on the immature mind, an experience which is remembered merely as a day of well wishing and gifts. Thus our kerygma must more and more rely on trust in the constant power of the sacramental character in our lives, that character which is dispensed in confirmation. We nourish this trust by inculcating a deep awareness in the faithful of the essence of confirmation as a fulfillment of baptism.

The grace of confirmation also finds its source in the incarnation of the Logos. Cyril of Jerusalem has given the kerygma of confirmation its classic expression by pointing up the relationship between the birth of baptism and the anointing of confirmation: "Since you were baptized in Christ and put on Christ you have become one in form with the Son of God. Since God has previously destined us for adoption he made us equal in the glorified body of Christ. After you have held a share in the anointed, you are then rightfully called anointed . . . [for] you have received the image of the Spirit. . . . The Christos was anointed with the spiritual oil of joy, that is, with the Holy Spirit, who as the source of joy is called the 'oil of joy,' so that you too may be anointed with the myrrh from which you may be called participators and companions in Christ." Even today the Greek Church calls the sacrament of confirmation "the myrrh."

In the incarnation the Logos was anointed according to his human nature. As St. Augustine has said, "God anointed him with the Holy Spirit (Acts 10, 38). The Church anoints the baptized not only with the visible oil, but also with the gift of grace which is signified by the visible ointment."[10] Through the incarnation all of mankind is bound together in a new unity. "He is the leaven, while you are the mass of dough."[11] This bread can be kneaded together when sprinkled with the water of baptism, but it must be baked firm in the fire of the Spirit: "As yet there is no bread without fire. What, then, does fire signify? This is the chrism. For the oil of our fire, the Holy Spirit, is

---

[10] *De Trinitate*, XV, 26 (*PL* 38, 1100).
[11] *Catecheses*, III, 6 (*PG* 33, 1093a).

the sacrament."[12] The Church Fathers always return to this point: that the strengthening-anointing with the myrrh effects in the baptized the maturity of the body of Christ in the power of the spiritual anointing of the incarnation, a growing unto death. Because the sacrificial death of the God-man is at the same time the decisive split with the diabolical mystery of evil, confirmation is as much an anointing for battle as for death.

Confirmation is the anointing to death. The Spirit is poured out because the Lord is glorified in death (Jn. 7, 39). Since this promise of the Spirit is given to all the faithful, it indubitably signifies a prophecy of confirmation. The great piercing which Zechariah prophesied is the one which "will pour out of the Spirit of grace and prayer over the house of David and the inhabitants of Jerusalem" (Zech. 12, 10; Apoc. 1, 7). The remembrance of the ordination unto death of the incarnation which is found in our prayers has its value in the mystical body of Christ, which emerged from the virginal birth of baptism: "You come out from the sacrarium of the Virgin as an uncontaminated victim." The increase of baptismal grace is essentially a progression towards the cross. Therefore, martydom is the epitome of the anointing of the Spirit. "As in natural life, generation and growing are different, so too baptism—which contains the power of rebirth in itself—is to be distinguished from confirmation. It is through the power of confirmation that the faithful grow and acquire the complete strength of the Spirit, and strengthened with this power they cannot be intimidated from the confession of faith through fear of penalties, dangers, martyrdom, or death."[13]

The death of Christ was glorification. It was the "casting out of the prince of this world (Jn. 12, 31; 16, 11), through a victory which disarmed him of his powers and authority (Col. 2, 15). Glorification is the trophy of the final war. For this reason the confirming bishop says, "I sign you with the sign of the cross and confirm you with the chrism of salvation." The cross is the visible sign of the sacramental character in the fighters of the

[12] St. Augustine, *Sermo*, 227 (*PL* 38, 1100).
[13] *Roman Catechism*, II, 3, 6.

200

Lord who "are led out from the hidden protection of the Church onto the battlefield. It is the sign under which the Christian has fought and won," says St. Thomas. Therefore, confirmation is the sacrament of Christian heroism. As far as the aspect of conflict is concerned, we can avoid speaking with intolerable pathos only if we properly grasp the kerygma about Satan and his kingdom. The man who wants to retain his spiritual life after baptism and also his spiritual mission, must keep fighting against the enemy of the spiritual life and Christian faith. The spiritual life of man is therefore one of spiritual combat. It is for this reason that the baptized are conferred with the strengthening divine grace of confirmation.

Throughout the entire tradition of the Fathers we find this idea taken up: that confirmation is a growing into the manhood of Christ, into full responsibility in the kingdom of God; that it is a growing unto death and then to glorification—a growing not only through waging war against Satan, but also by participating in the definitively won victory. Confirmation, as the sacrament in which our faith is strengthened, is not merely a sacrament of this life, but by its indelible character it is essentially projected into the glory of the life to come. This is so because Christ has already won the decisive victory.

St. Leo the Great has called confirmation the sign of eternal life. It is given to us, according to St. Ambrose, "so that we might possess his splendor, and thus his image [the Holy Spirit], and grace, which is truly a spiritual sign."[14] In our kerygma we must help the baptized faithful understand that their confirmation is an anointing unto death, and that therefore it is a participation in the priesthood of the Anointed, who in the immolation of the cross effects the glory of the resurrection of the flesh.

We come now to two sacraments of this life, penance and the anointing of the sick. These sacraments dispense graces which are essentially different from the two character-imprinting sacraments of baptism and confirmation, but they are profoundly necessary in the salvific order of Christ. The dispensing of divine

14 *De Spiritu Sancto,* I, 6 (*PL* 16, 723).

life is no longer given to the race as such through the mystery of the descendancy from Adam, but to each man individually (even though as members of the mystical body) in the sacrament of baptism. The preternatural gifts that are necessarily tied up with sanctifying grace are not given back to the individual baptized but will be given at the end of the world. Therefore, the body of Christ is now built from mysteries that are impressed through a sign. Although the decisive victory is already won, it is possible for the individual members to lose the mysteriously hidden glory, that is, to sin. In the chapter of the *Summa Contra Gentiles* which treats of both of these redeeming sacraments, St. Thomas inaugurates a profound inquiry into the possibilities for sinning in the blessed body of Christ (IV, 70). When from the point of view of the mystery of the body of Christ and eternal life we try to join both of these sacraments into the cosmos of the sacraments, we must say that much of the victory of glorification was given to the whole body of Christ through his priestly sacrificial death. Now the mystery of glory is fulfilled in our mortal flesh. It is also correct to say with the apostle (2 Thess. 2, 7) that the mystery of evil is still in effect.

Our kerygma must continually teach the faithful to grasp these unusual deeds in their entirety, realizing all the while the extraordinary difficulties involved: that it is possible to lose the love of the Trinity, the rebirth in the Holy Spirit, and the regal priestly anointing; also that we can be worthy of the original power of grace which God has decided upon, and that we can be confronted with this renewed break of the diabolical with the visible grace-effecting signs. There is a trace of holy astonishment in the plain words with which Thomas Aquinas sets forth the necessity of the sacrament of penance: "The overflowing completeness of the divine mercy and the authority of the grace of Christ could not allow that a baptized person who has committed sin after baptism not be freed through a second baptism, but cast out without the forgiveness of sins."[15] So it was that Christ instituted two sacraments and with Thomas we call them

---

[15] *Summa Contra Gentiles*, IV, 72.

the "spiritual healing" (penance) and the "completion of the entire spiritual cure" (anointing of the sick) (extreme unction). Both belong close together because both ought either heal or protect the wounded member of the body of Christ as long as this earthly visibility covers the lost or endangered glory. Trent, too, showed the inner relationship of these two sacraments when it said: "This sacrament of extreme unction is the completed conclusion not only of the sacrament of penance but of the whole Christian life, which ought to be a constant penance" (D. 907).

Without doubt, our present-day kerygma on penance is formed by two points above all: the difficult question of the internal reason for the historical development of the early Christian confessional practice and the modern confession of devotion, and the question of the all too painful visibility of the dispensation of grace through the generally compulsive "confessive institute" which was bound up with confession and the humanity of the absolving priest. But it seems to us that the theology of the visible and our constant endeavor to join the sacraments to the great line of salvation history which leads to the coming glory in the body of Christ can be particularly meaningful precisely regarding these two questions.

First of all, in our kerygma we ought to show the deep relationship which the sacrament of penance has with the source of all the sacraments, the incarnation of the Logos. Christ himself uttered the words of institution for this sacrament: "As my Father has sent me, so I send you" (Jn. 20, 21). From the lofty theology of the Johannine gospel, which never tires of speaking of this "being sent through the Father" (4, 34; 5, 23; 7, 16. 29. 33; 8, 16. 29; 10, 36; 11, 42; 17, 3. 18. 20), we learn of the human heart of Jesus, the Saviour who "saved his people from sin" (Mt. 1, 21), who was completely aware of the fact that he was the one who was "sent" from the bosom of the Father and so must lead men back to the Father, to the divine origin of his own nature. This "sending" found its beginning in the incarnation, in the mission of human suffering which destroyed sin through the power of the eternal birth from the

203

Father. Therefore, this power to forgive sin also takes its source from the incarnation and from the "today I have begotten you" of this sacrificial becoming a priest. The infinitely deep love which through the Holy Spirit formed the body of the Saviour from the Virgin continues in the mystical body of Christ. This is so much true that this sin-quenching power whose source is the Spirit not only signifies a once-in-a-lifetime salvation in baptism, but embraces the "sins of the world." Above all, it drives out all that is always sinful in the body of Christ through the storm of the Spirit.

But since the incarnation this Spirit has become visible in the sacrificial body, born of the Virgin, and in the humble body of the visible Church. This visibility of the Spirit should now be continued in those who are sent as Christ was sent by the Father. It should also perdure in the breath that Christ whispers to the man who has been signed in order to dispense the divine Pneuma through the perishable passing breath of a poor human word. It is in this way that he allows the flood which is the source of invisible grace to pour out at every call of a baptized man, from the continually pierced side of the mystical body of Christ.

Thus the sacrament of penance comes to the "hearer of the Spirit" as it came on the first Pentecost, when the first believers confessed and "saved them from this condemned flesh" (Acts 2, 38–40). The sacrament of penance is the procession of the eternal Word from the Father, which is to the whispered words of man a boundless stream that fructifies the desert sands of our visibility with the living water of the Spirit. "As my Father has sent me . . ." "Receive the Holy Spirit . . ." It is in this that the mystery of this sacrament is hidden at the same time as its sacramental effect is spoken: to instill once again the Trinitarian life in the heart of the penitent and to continue the holy construction of the mystical body of Christ. This is the same body which was once "sent by the Father" and which was formed by the power of the Holy Spirit.

Our kerygma of penance must now try to unravel the questions mentioned above. The often painful human visibility in which this sacrament is effected must now be placed as a powerful cornerstone of our building of the theology of the visible. We have rigorously prepared the stones in our kerygmatic construct, and the humanity of the sacrament of penance must fortify it. To our mind, the external form of this sacrament unfolding in an ever more distinct "audibility of the Spirit" is simply the exercise of the inalienable claim of the visible Church concerning the judicial law that all mortal sins must be submitted to the forum of the visible sacrament. As for the "confession of devotion," we must keep in mind that confession is in the end an act of God which destroys our sins, and that only by confessing his sins can a man discover a merciful, forgiving God. Devotional confession is simply a form of sacramental penitential asceticism. Each confession is the sacramental anticipation of that time of illustrious victory "when the Lord Jesus will slay with the breath of his mouth and will destroy with the brightness of his glory" (2 Thess. 2, 8). Confession emanates from the wounded side of the Lord, and at the same time is the sacrament of glory. It is the breath by which the Pneuma leads the baptized towards the day of victory.

It is precisely here that the sacrament of ordination to death, or the anointing of the sick, fits in, for incarnation is the anointing unto death. Salvation is effected through the free participation of the God-man in the disintegration of the visible in death—which is natural to the human race. Since the fall, man is no longer taken care of by preternatural gifts. Therefore, the death of one baptized in Christ, as it is taught in the theology of the Epistle to the Romans, is a great mystery, a final distinction between victory or defeat. Certainly this is so in comparison to the murdered God-man, who conquered death in death. That instant of death, where all the mysteries of Christianity are massed together, had to be elevated into the scope of a visible sacrament, through which grace is dispensed according to God's plan of salvation. The attainable encounter with God in the sacred sign can now once again be fulfilled in the natural disintegration of the visible. The anointing of the sick is, as we know, a sacrament of the living, it first of all effects what is meaningfully indicated in the sign, namely, the strengthening Spirit anointing with sanctifying grace, the "easier raising up" of which James speaks (Jas. 5, 15), the last anointing for battle (D. 907). It blots out the remaining sins by itself (and not in the way that the other sacraments of the living do)—presupposing the proper disposition. Peculiar to this sacrament is that double character which points it out as an ordination for death. In that instant when all is decisively chosen, when the mystery of the death-suffering of Christ is once again illumined for the member of his body who is ordained to die, death is seen as a victory over Satan and a passage to glory. The basic structure of this sacrament is fastened together by both terms, body of Christ and eternal life, salvation and glorification. As St. Thomas has said, "This sacrament is the last one and in a certain way it is the consummation of all spiritual care, by which man is partially prepared for participation in eternal glory."[16]

Finally, we must treat of the loftiest of all the sacraments, the mystery of the Eucharist. The brevity with which we do so has no relation to how we ought to fashion our complete kerygmatic theology. In our preaching on the Eucharist we will find the words of Aquinas of great use: *"nec laudare sufficis."* We have come to speak more and more of this sacrament, built with a kind of secretiveness. The body of Christ and eternal life, visibility and invisibility, are not hidden in this mystery according to their grace-effecting power, but are truly real and essentially present in the glorified sacrificial body of the Logos. "For in baptism the incarnate Word is contained only according to a virtue, but in the sacrament of the Eucharist we confess that he himself is contained according to substance," says St. Thomas.[17] Therefore, all the other sacraments have a deeply interior tendency towards this mystery. Aquinas has presented this truth in a most beautiful way, progressing from holy orders, baptism, and confirmation, and joining penance and the anoint-

16 *Ibid.,* IV, 73.
17 *Ibid.,* 61.

ing of the sick together, and annexing matrimony. We endeavored to copy this pattern in our kerygmatic construct. The Eucharist is the ultimate goal and crowning glory of all the sacraments, the end and perfection of the sacraments. It is the divinely sacred visible sign which lies hidden in the depths of the Godhead, and which has found its fulfillment in the Church, in the salvific love of the Trinity whose love has become visible. "In this sacrament the total mystery of our salvation is comprehended," says St. Thomas.[18]

The sacrament of the Eucharist is a sacrifice. It is a grace-giving sacrament and the perduring presence of the Lord. These three points of view truly ought to be kept distinguished one from the other, and their delicately structured interrelationship ought not be ruptured by the arbitrary action of a careless piety.

Even in this divine sacrament our kerygma must proceed from the fact that the Eucharist is a sacrifice. The granting of grace and the perduring presence are fruits of the sacrifice. Now it is apparent that, with real dogmatic justification, we let all the doctrine on the sacraments proceed from the sacrifice of the God-man, from his high priesthood. In his chapter on the priesthood in the *Summa Contra Gentiles* St. Thomas says, "Therefore, since the power of ordination is directed towards the dispensing of the sacraments and because among the sacraments the loftiest and overabundantly complete sacrament is the Eucharist, the priestly power must be treated primarily with an eye to this mystery."[19] The soul of our kerygma must be the holy sacrifice of the Mass, and we cannot properly speak of that without first of all recalling once again all that we explained earlier about sacrifice and the characteristics of sacrifice. But the sacrifice of the Mass must be led back to the ordination unto death of the incarnation, to the glorification of the immolative death on the cross. It is this same sacrifice on the cross which is offered through the priest at Mass (D. 940). "Our Lord God had at one time wanted to offer himself

---

[18] *Summa Theologica*, III, q. 83, a. 4c.
[19] IV, 74.

on the altar of the cross as a sacrifice to the Father in order
to effect the eternal salvation for all those who want to attain
to the fulfillment of sanctity. But because through his death
he did not want his priesthood to end, he wanted, at that
last meal on the night of his betrayal, to leave to his beloved
bride the Church a visible sacrifice. He desired that the bloody
sacrifice which once was brought about on the cross become
his perpetual remembrance until the end of time" (D. 938).
In these words are summed up all the the mysteries of Christian preaching: the holy sacrifice of the Mass is truly the
quintessence of the revealed mysteries. We cannot understand
the sacrifice without speaking about the Logos who gives the
salvific power to the sacrifice of men; without speaking about
the Spirit who descends at the call of his Church to transform
the offerings. In the sacrifice of mediation the whole work
of redemption, from the incarnation until the death on the
cross, is mystically repeated. In sacrifice the Church is perpetually born anew. The sacrifice is, finally, "Preaching of
the death of the Lord until he returns once again" (1 Cor. 11,
36). That is, the sacrifice is not only the perdurance of the
destruction of the visible, but at the same time it is also
the perduring of the glorified coming of the Lord, the everlasting parousia. In the main eucharistic prayer of the early
Roman Church the sacrificing priest prayed: "We give you
thanks, Oh God, through your beloved servant, Jesus Christ,
whom you have sent us in the last times as Saver and Saviour,
as the messenger of your will who is your inseparable Logos,
through whom you have created all in order to find your
pleasure in all. You have sent him from heaven into the
maternal womb of the Virgin, from whom he took his flesh . . .
born of the Holy Spirit and the Virgin. Your will fulfilling,
he wanted to acquire a holy people, he stretched his hands
out in suffering in order to save the believers by his sufferings.
As he freely gave himself over to suffering, in order to conquer
death, to loose the bonds of Satan, to crush out hell, to illumine
the righteous, to establish a cornerstone . . . he took bread,
thanked you and said: 'Take you and eat: this is my body' . . ."

The eucharistic sacrifice is the "cornerstone," the trophy of the final victory over Satan, the bond between time and eternity, the sign of the Kyrios who "can no longer die" (Rom. 6, 9).

The second point of reference in our preaching of the sacrament of Eucharist is that the Eucharist is a grace-effecting sign which "effects what it signifies." The food will be taken and eaten at the sacrificial altar, and it is here that its meaning is found (and also its effect): as a sacrificial food it is also a body-building nourishment. Therefore, it is united with the sacrificial, and through the sacrifice with the glorified body of Christ to the construction of his permanent mystical body of glory in the "unity with Christ" (D. 691). But our own kerygma must form a unity which is richer and more tangible, and so it ought to make use of all of the theology which we have discussed up to this point. Communion is the unity with him who was born of the eternal Father: "As the living Father has sent me, and as I live because of the Father, so he who eats me, he also shall live because of me" (Jn. 6, 57). Communion is participation in the incarnation and in the body sacrificed in death on the cross from whose sufferings and earthly wound the Church is built. It is, therefore, the "sacrament of Church unity," as Thomas Aquinas says.[20] Communion is participation in the already glorified body of Christ. It is the incursion of the parousia under the concealed form of the sacrificial offering, and thus it is the sacrament of the resurrection of the body. "Bond of the coming glory and never ending happiness," as Trent states (D. 875).

After we have preached of the Eucharist as sacrifice and as the grace-giving food from the sacrificial altar, we can then form the dogmatically correct and deeper kerygma of the unceasing presence of the eucharistic Lord. Christ is present on the altar as one who is sacrificed, as he is glorified in the ever repeated and complete mystical sacrifice. "Christ is not enthroned in the tabernacle, but he kneels," is a way that we can briefly point out this extremely important kerygmatic

---

[20] *Summa Theologica*, III, q. 79, a. 1c; see q. 67, a. 2c; q. 73, a. 4c.

application. His presence is not there for its own sake but with the pressing goal of unity in communion, and this in turn for the reason of the construction of the body of Christ and for the glorification in the Father. The Lord is not "quietly enclosed in the tabernacle," but in the quiet of the Church, in the silence of the adorer who is fulfilled by the "loud-crying mysteries" in the host exposed in the monstrance which once would be brought forth in the stillness of God. He is fulfilled by the all-powerful desire which presses on the human heart of the Logos: to return to the Father!

Thus it now remains for us to speak of the journey of all flesh to the heart of the eternal Father.

CHAPTER TWELVE

THE RESURRECTION OF THE FLESH

Telos is the last thing only in the order of time. In the order of things it is always present and begins its powerful work at the very beginning of things. Eschatology is the heart of Christian preaching. Christianity is God becoming flesh in the incarnation, in the Church, and in the sacraments (beginning with the sanctification of human procreation and ending with the body of Christ born of the Virgin, on the sacrificial altar). The Word flushed with victory is the essence of Christian eschatology.

There was and is still a Monophysitism of the mystical body of Christ. Spiritual men of all times have not always been able to grasp what the Church of Christ (and we with her) prays to the Father: "Having united himself with the substance of our fragility, he put it at his right hand in glory." They focused their considerations on the end of the history of salvation, on the never-ending beginning of eternity in the truly spiritual way that the angels do. The result was that the secret ideal of ascetics and piety became the "angelic life." Even for the mystical body we must once again contrast this idea with that very meaningful hymn which was first intoned by the Council of Chalcedon. "We believe in one and the same Christ, the Son, the Lord, the only-born who has two natures, unmixed, unchanging, unbroken, and unvarying." In the divinized participation of our flesh in the sonship in Christ to the Father this flesh is not absorbed in the Spirit but now remains for all eternity, even though our flesh is spiritualized, glorified, and illumined by the divine light and is "placed with

211

Christ in God" (Col. 3, 4) in the kingdom of heaven (Eph. 2, 6). "Our lowliness is taken up in glorification, our weakness is taken up in power, and our mortality in eternity, in him who in his invisible nature becomes visible among our people," says Leo the Great in his dogmatic letter (D. 143, 144). As the Logos will never put aside his flesh, so too our flesh glorified in Christ will never lose his nature.

"His kingdom will never end" defined the first Council of Constantinople (D. 86) against the heresy of Marcellus of Ankara, who stated that at the end of time the Logos would once again return into the Trinity. He believed that the unity with the human body is merely an episode in the history of salvation. Cyril of Jerusalem countered with the following: "If you should sometime hear that the kingdom of Christ has an end, then hate this heresy! It is a new monster that has just reared its ugly head in Galatia. Someone has the boldness to preach that Christ will no longer reign supreme after the end of the world, and is bold enough to assert that the Logos, who went out from the Father, will then melt back again into the Father and no longer exist."[1] Augustine uses sharp words when he fights against this spiritualized meaning, through which the precious hope of all Christian belief would be basically destroyed. "No one believes that the appearance of Christ which took on a human created nature will later revert back into the divinity, or to speak more precisely, into the Godhead which is in no way created, but into the unity in the Trinity, established, bodiless, and unconverted . . . nature."[2] Therefore, the most important thing that our kerygma must take up, with a holy passion, relates to the last things. It is the mission of the resurrection of our flesh: "The fidelity of Christians, the resurrection of the dead," says Tertullian.[3] Our preaching must be formed in the light of the present world, heaven and hell, and the new world and the vision of the triune God.

[1] *Catecheses*, XV, 27 (*PG* 33, 909a-b).
[2] *De Trinitate*, I, 8, 15 (*PL* 42, 829).
[3] *De Carnis Resurrectione*, 1.

"We profess that with Christ, our head, as a prototype, all of the dead will come to a true resurrection of the flesh. But we do not believe that we will arise in a different body but in this one in which we live, remain, and move around. The holy catholic Church that he established at the price of his blood will reign supreme with him in heaven. In our living hearts we believe and hold fast to the resurrection of the dead and wait the joy of the coming times." So exclaims the wonderful profession which the early Spanish Church set up against Priscillian asceticism (D. 287). The Lateran Council traces this idea back to the festive but hard truths on heaven and hell. Living and dead, damned and chosen, "will all arise with the same body which they had here in order to receive, the one eternal punishment with the devil, the other eternal glory with Christ, each according to his good or bad works" (D. 429). Once again we must return to the beginning of this glorification of the flesh, to the incarnation of the Logos. We must profess with St. Thomas, "First the Word of God grants immortal life to the body joined naturally with him, and through it brings the resurrection to all the others."[4] This Logos and his holy revivifying Spirit which was poured out over all flesh through the death of the God-man, who lives in the Church, will revitalize our flesh and make it incorruptible for the glorification in God the Father. That, briefly, is the compendium of the lofty theology of the resurrection of the body as Irenaeus has presented it to us. Thus our kerygma must be thoroughly worked out from the ultimate meaning of all theology of the visible, and it must extend this theology to the mystery-filled truths about the "new world," about the "reformation of the world" and the "new earth and new heaven" (Mt. 19, 28; 2 Pet. 3, 13; Apoc. 21).

St. Paul reminds us that "the coming world" is already in effect, that "the power of the coming aeon is already upon us" (Heb. 6, 5), and St. Peter tells us that the "day breaks and the sun comes up in our hearts" (2 Pet. 1, 19). The coming

---

[4] *Summa Theologica*, III, q. 56, a. 1c.

light of glory is already growing in our hearts because we already "had Christ in us," who is the hope of glory (Col. 1, 27). What we have to preach in order to bring out the paradox is the "eschatology of the present." St. Paul did this without ever letting up. Because Christ and his Spirit are already in us, our flesh is already dead, but in and through this death our spirit begins to become lightened in the glory which proceeds from that Spirit which Christ awakens through his death. This lightening which the Spirit brings to the soul will some day revivify our corpses with glory. Even now the Spirit of glorification lives in us. That is the doctrine contained in the Epistle to the Romans (8, 10, 11). From this truth comes the sentence which is so frequently misunderstood: "The bodies of this time cannot be compared with the coming glory which shall be revealed to us" (Rom. 8, 18). There is no longer only the relationship (although there is one) of a work performed and its reward, but through the body itself, through the wearing out and the daily dying, man enters even more deeply into the "glorious freedom of the child of God" (Rom. 8, 21). He is together with creation which in him and with him should at some time participate in glory. At the end of our kerygmatic formulation of the revealed truths we can once more, by the strength of the eschatology, illuminate the most urgent blessed facts of our Christian earthly lives. They are the suffering and life in Christ, the participation in his destruction of everything visible till the destruction of death, and the participation in his divinity in the Holy Spirit of glory. All human suffering is a mystery that becomes reasonable in the light of the last things. All human suffering accepted in Christ or chosen with loving free will presently leads to that glorification which we call mystic and which is mysteriously and darkly yet vividly experienced. Body and mystic, cross and Spirit, blood and living water, all of these belong together since the Spirit was poured out from a pierced heart onto all flesh. In the destruction of the *corpus humilitatis* in the resignation of the earthly and the dwelling in the heavenly, our glorification is constructed. Then our poor bodies will have the

214

same shape as the body of his glory (Phil. 3, 20–21). The visible must pass on, must die like a grain of wheat, for Christ the Lord is still "hidden in God" (Col. 3, 3). "Nothing which is here visible is good because our God, Jesus Christ, appears much more joyous since he returned to the Father," says Ignatius the martyr (*Rom.* 3, 3). The world has crucified him and in so doing washed him with the water which leads to the returning home to the Father (*Rom.* 7, 2). We come then to the happy end of all the theology of the visible which we have treated with much care. We also come to the divine and Christian paradox. The visible must die, it must become invisible for a little while, just as Christ hid himself for a little while in the bosom of the Father in order to be revealed in his glory. "It is beautiful (as the sun) to take my departure and rise up to God so that I may have my own sunrise in God," writes Ignatius (*Rom.* 2, 2). But a secret and valuable glimpse of the coming glory can be found in the destruction of the visible. One can already "see and hear" the Spirit, he can "touch" the invisible Logos even in his mystical body. They become mature, kindly, and radiant in the great love, sanctity, and suffering which takes on a new meaning, through which the divine can be grasped. It is the fragrance of the Spirit, the distant sound of the rushing water of eternity. Earthly love is blind to the things of the Spirit, but heavenly love, the love from the Holy Spirit to the Father which offers itself, which participates in the priestly immolation on the cross of the Logos, who was born of the Virgin, obtains for us here below the illumined sense, the "qualified" meaning (Heb. 4, 14). Through it we can see the Spirit in the midst of the blind visibility. "For worldly delights do not have the invisible eyes through which the Holy Spirit can be seen. If they could not be invisible . . . yet they seem invisible."[5] Thus does St. Augustine quite precisely join our theology of the visible and the invisible to the eschatology of the present, the eschatology of asceticism and the mystic.

[5] *In Joannem,* 74, 4–5 (*PL* 35, 1828–1829).

We close this all too brief and fleeting attempt to reconstruct our theology which the lofty words of St. Paul gave us in his preaching: "Even though our outer man is decaying, yet our inner man is being renewed day by day. For our present light affliction, which is passing, prepares for us an eternal measure of glory that is beyond earthly measure. We must contemplate not merely these things which are visible, but all those things which are not visible to the eye. For the things that are visible to the eye are temporal, and those things which are not visible to the eye are eternal" (2 Cor. 4, 16–18).

216